76 Fallacies

By Dr. Michael C. LaBossiere

First Print Edition 2013

Table of Contents

About the Author

Dr. Michael LaBossiere is a runner from Maine who went to school in Ohio and ended up a philosophy professor in Florida.

While acquiring his doctorate in philosophy at Ohio State University, he earned his ramen noodle money by writing for Chaosium, GDW, R. Talsorian Games, and TSR. After graduate school, he became a philosophy professor at Florida A&M University. His first philosophy book, *What Don't You Know?*, was published in 2008. He continues to write philosophy and gaming material. He is also a blogger, but these days who isn't?

When not writing, he enjoys running, gaming and the martial arts. Thanks to a quadriceps tendon tear in 2009, he was out of running for a while, but returned to the trails and wrote a book about it, *Of Tendon & Trail*. He can be contacted at ontologist@aol.com. His Amazon author page is at http://amazon.com/author/michaellabossiere.

Introduction

In addition to combining the content of *42 Fallacies* and *30 More Fallacies*, this book features some revisions as well as a new section on common formal fallacies.

As the title indicates, this book presents seventy six fallacies. The focus is on providing the reader with definitions and examples of these common fallacies rather than being a handbook on winning arguments or general logic. Understanding what a fallacy is requires that you first have at least a basic understanding of arguments in the philosophical sense. In philosophy, an argument is not a fight or even a dispute. Rather, an argument is as set of claims (statements that can be true or false) that are related in a way that one of them is supported by the others. Another way to look at it is that one claim is presented to be proven and the other claims are presented as evidence or reasons for that claim,

In technical terms, the claim being argued for is known as the conclusion. A single argument has one (and only one) conclusion. One way to spot a conclusion is to ask "what is the point that is supposed to be proven here?" If there is no point, then there is no argument. Of course, a person can make a point without offering proof, so what is also needed is evidence or reasons. The evidence or reasons being presented in support of the conclusion are known as premises. An argument will always have at least one premise, but there is no limit on the number allowed. One way to find premises is to ask "what reasons, if any, are being given in support of the conclusion?" If no reasons are given, then there is no argument present.

In general, philosophers take arguments to be of two main types: deductive and inductive. A deductive argument is an argument such that the premises provide (or are supposed to provide) complete support for the conclusion. An inductive argument is an argument such that the premises provide (or are supposed to provide) some degree of support (but less than complete support) for the conclusion. The support given by the premises to the conclusion is a matter of logic and, interestingly enough, has nothing to do with whether the premises are actually true or not. I will say more about this later.

If a deductive argument's premises properly support the conclusion, the argument is valid. In technical terms, a valid deductive argument is such that if all its premises were true, then its conclusion must be true.

If a deductive argument is valid and actually does have all true premises, then it is sound. An argument can be valid and unsound by having one or more false premises.

If a deductive argument is such that the premises could all be true while the conclusion is false at the same time, then the argument is invalid. Invalid arguments are always unsound. This is because a sound argument must be valid and have all true premises.

An invalid argument is also known as a formal fallacy or a deductive fallacy. This book includes some of the classic named deductive fallacies.

Deductive arguments are tested for validity using a variety of methods, such as Venn diagrams, truth tables and logical proofs. While these are interesting (well, to some people), they will not be covered in this book.

Inductive arguments are assessed differently from deductive arguments. If the premises of an inductive argument support the conclusion adequately (or better) it is a strong argument. It is such that if the premises are true, the conclusion is likely to be true. If a strong inductive argument has all true premises, it is sometimes referred to as being cogent.

One feature of inductive logic is that even a strong inductive argument can have a false conclusion even when all the premises are true. This is because of what is known as the inductive leap: with an inductive argument the conclusion always goes beyond the premises. However, this does not make all inductive reasoning fallacious (although it does make it all technically invalid). An inductive fallacy occurs when an argument's premises do not adequately support the conclusion. In most fallacies this occurs because the premises being offered have little or no logical connection to conclusion. The fallacies covered in this book are of the informal inductive sort.

Before moving on to the actual fallacies, it is necessary to have a short discussion about what fallacies are not. Unfortunately for those who teach about fallacies, people often use the term "fallacy" when they are actually referring to a factual error. For example, someone might say "a lot of people think that Google created Android from scratch, but that is a fallacy. Google actually based Android on

Linux." While thinking that Android was created from scratch would be an error, it is an error about the facts, rather than an error in logic. If someone said "Android is awful. After all, a fair number of creepy geeks use it", then this would be an error in logic. Even if creepy geeks use Android, this does not prove that the operating system is awful. While both of these are mistakes, they are two different types of mistakes.

To see why, think about balancing a checkbook. I can make a mistake by doing the math incorrectly (which would be an error in reasoning) and I can make a mistake by entering the wrong amount for a check. These errors are different and treating them the same would cause confusion. The same applies for fallacies and factual errors.

To use another analogy, think about cooking. One way I could screw up a meal is by cooking badly. This would be like an error in logic. Another way is that I could use the wrong (or bad) ingredients. That would be like making a factual error.

As such, it is one thing to get the facts wrong (factual error) and quite another to reason badly about them (fallacy).

So, a fallacy is an error in reasoning/logic. To be more specific, a fallacy is an argument in which the premises fail to provide adequate logical support for the conclusion. A deductive fallacy, as noted above, is a deductive argument that is invalid (it is such that it could have all true premises and still have a false conclusion). Whether an argument is valid or invalid is an objective matter and can be tested by various means, such as truth tables and proofs.

An inductive fallacy is less formal than a deductive fallacy. They are weak inductive arguments in which the premises do not provided enough support for the conclusion. While deductive arguments can be tested with objective and definitive means, the same is not true for inductive arguments. There are objective standards, but assessing informal fallacies is somewhat like judging figure skating: really good and really bad cases are easy to spot, but there are situations where there will be reasonable dispute.

People also use the term "fallacy" to refer to errors that are not factual errors and do not involve actual arguments (in the technical sense). This is sometimes done when referring to cases of rhetoric in which an argument is not present. Some people are rather flexible about what counts as a fallacy and include things that more strict classifiers would exclude. My approach is to present the fallacies in terms of being flawed arguments while also respecting the broader usage of the term by mentioning such common uses in the relevant fallacies.

When reading through the fallacies, be sure to keep in mind that there is no "official governing body" for fallacies. As such, you will almost certainly see other names and slightly different definitions for these fallacies in other sources.

It is also a good idea to keep in mind that not all things that look like fallacies are actually fallacies. In some cases, they are not fallacies because they are not arguments. In other cases, what might be taken as a fallacy is actually a non-fallacious argument. I have taken care to make a special note of such cases in the relevant descriptions. As a final point, there are far more fallacies than are listed in this book (or any book). So, just because something does not match a named fallacy, it might still be a fallacy (or it might not).

Examples

Example of a Valid Deductive Argument
Premise 1: If Bill is a cat, then Bill is a mammal.
Premise 2: Bill is a cat.
Conclusion: Bill is a mammal.

Example of a Strong Inductive Argument
Premise 1: The vast majority of American cats are domestic house cats.
Premise 2: Bill is an American cat.
Conclusion: Bill is domestic house cat.

Example of a Factual Error
Columbus, Ohio is the capital of the United States.

Example of a Deductive Fallacy (an Invalid Deductive Argument)
Premise 1: If Portland is the capital of Maine, then it is in Maine.
Premise 2: Portland is in Maine.
Conclusion: Portland is the capital of Maine.
(Portland is in Maine, but Augusta is the capital.)

Example of an Inductive Fallacy (a Hasty Generalization)
Premise 1: Having just arrived in Ohio, I saw a white squirrel.
Conclusion: All Ohio squirrels are white.

Fallacies and Arguments

In order to understand what a fallacy is, one must understand what an argument is. Very briefly an argument consists of one or more premises and one conclusion. A premise is a statement (a sentence that is either true or false) that is offered in support of the claim being made, which is the conclusion (which is also a sentence that is either true or false).

There are two main types of arguments: deductive and inductive. A deductive argument is an argument such that the premises provide (or appear to provide) complete support for the conclusion. An inductive argument is an argument such that the premises provide (or appear to provide) some degree of support (but less than complete support) for the conclusion. If the premises actually provide the required degree of support for the conclusion, then the argument is a good one. A good deductive argument is known as a valid argument and is such that if all its premises are true, then its conclusion must be true. If all the argument is valid and actually has all true premises, then it is known as a sound argument. If it is invalid or has one or more false premises, it will be unsound. A good inductive argument is known as a strong (or "cogent") inductive argument. It is such that if the premises are true, the conclusion is likely to be true.

A fallacy is, very generally, an error in reasoning. This differs from a factual error, which is simply being wrong about the facts. To be more specific, a fallacy is an "argument" in which the premises given for the conclusion do not provide the needed degree of support. A deductive fallacy is a deductive argument that is invalid (it is such that it could have all true premises and still have a false conclusion). An inductive fallacy is less formal than a deductive fallacy. They are simply "arguments" which appear to be inductive arguments, but the premises do not provided enough support for the conclusion. In such cases, even if the premises were true, the conclusion would not be more likely to be true.

Examples
Example of a Deductive Argument
Premise 1: If Bill is a cat, then Bill is a mammal.
Premise 2: Bill is a cat.
Conclusion: Bill is a mammal.

Example of an Inductive Argument
Premise 1: Most American cats are domestic house cats.
Premise 2: Bill is an American cat.
Conclusion: Bill is domestic house cat.

Example of a Factual Error
Columbus is the capital of the United States.

Example of a Deductive Fallacy
Premise 1: If Portland is the capital of Maine, then it is in Maine.
Premise 2: Portland is in Maine.

Conclusion: Portland is the capital of Maine.
(Portland is in Maine, but Augusta is the capital. Portland is the largest city in Maine, though.)

Example of an Inductive Fallacy
Premise 1: Having just arrived in Ohio, I saw a white squirrel.
Conclusion: All Ohio squirrels are white.
(While there are many, many squirrels in Ohio, the white ones are very rare).

Informal Fallacies

What you will find below are entries for the fallacies. Each entry provides a common name for the fallacy, common alternative names (if applicable), a general form, a description and examples.

Accent, Fallacy of

Description:
This fallacy occurs when a conclusion is drawn from a premise or premises that are ambiguous due to a lack of clarity regarding the emphasis. Most commonly this fallacy involves an ambiguity arising from a shift in emphasis/accent in the course of the argument. This fallacy has the following form:

1. Premises are presented that are ambiguous due to a lack of clarity regarding emphasis.
2. Conclusion C is drawn from these premises.

Ambiguity by itself is not fallacious, but is a lack of clarity in language that occurs when a claim has two (or more) meanings and it is not clear which is intended. The Fallacy of Accent occurs when an inference is drawn from a premise or premises on the basis of a specific sort of ambiguity that arises in three main ways.

The first is that a claim is ambiguous because the intended tone is not clear. For example, the claim "you would be lucky to get this person to work for you" could be high praise or a sarcastic remark depending on the tone used. The second is that the ambiguity arises from a lack of clarity regarding the intended stress. For example, the meaning of the claim "Leslie thinks that Sally has been faithful to him" can shift based on the stress. Stressed one way, the claim can be taken as indicating that Leslie thinks this, but is wrong. A third possibility is that claim is taken out of context. As an example, suppose that the original text was "Among the radical left, Mr. Jones has considerable appeal as a congressional candidate. However, mainstream voters rightfully regard him as a questionable choice, at best." If someone were to quote this as "Mr. Jones has considerable appeal as a congressional candidate", then they would be taking the quote out of context.

Perhaps the most used example of this sort of fallacy involves a hard drinking first mate and his teetotaler captain. Displeased by the mate's drinking habits, the captain always made a point of entering "the mate was drunk today" into the ship's log whenever the mate was drunk. One day, when the captain was sick, the mate entered "the captain was sober today" into the log. Naturally, the mate intended that the reader would take this emphasis as an indication that the event was unusual enough to be noted in the log and thus infer that the captain was drunk on all the other days. Obviously, to believe that conclusion would be to fall victim to the fallacy of accent.

Example #1

Sally: "I made Jane watch Jennifer Aniston in *Just Go With It* last night."
Ted: "What did she think?"
Sally: "She said that she never wants to see another Jennifer Aniston movie."
Ted: "But you love Jennifer and have all her movies. What are you going to do?"
Sally: "I'll do exactly what she said. I'll make her watch *Just Go With* it repeatedly."
Ted: "Cruel."
Sally: "Not at all. She did say that she never wants to see *another* Jennifer Aniston movie and I'll see to that by making sure that she watches that movie rather than another."

Example #2

Dr. Jane Gupta (on TV): "Though Prescott Pharmaceuticals claims that their VacsaDiet 3000 is 'guaranteed to help you shed those unsightly pounds', this claim has not been verified and many of the ingredients in the product present potential health risks."
Stephen: "Hey, Bob! Dr. Jane Gupta just said that 'Prescott Pharmaceuticals VacsaDiet 3000 is guaranteed to help you shed those unsightly pounds.'"
Bob: "In that case, I'm going to buy it. After all, Dr. Jane knows her stuff."
Stephen: "Yes she does. You just missed her-she was on TV talking all about diets and stuff."
Bob: "I'm sorry I missed that. By the way, do these new pants make me look fat?"
Stephen: "No, your fat makes you look fat."
Bob: "You wound me, sir."

Example #3

Employer: "I wasn't sure about hiring you. After all, you were at your last job just a month. But your former employer's letter said that anyone would be lucky to get you to work for them."

Keith: "I will do my best to live up to that, ma'am."

Employer: "I'm sure you will. Welcome to the company."

Accident, Fallacy of

Description:

This fallacy occurs when a general rule is misapplied to a specific case that is actually beyond its intended scope. The fallacy has the following form:

1. General rule G, which usually applies to Xs is presented.
2. A is an X, but is an exception to G.
3. G is applied to A as if it were not an exception.

This is an error in reasoning because the general rule is being incorrectly applied to the specific case at hand. The application is incorrect because of the accidental property or properties of X make it an exception to the rule.

This fallacy is historically attributed to Aristotle. As far as the name goes, it does not mean an accident in the usual sense (like getting hit by a car). Roughly put, Aristotle took an accidental property as lacking a necessary connection to the essence of a thing so that the property could change without the thing in question ceasing to be what it is. In contrast, essential qualities are necessary to the thing being what it is. For example, *having three sides* is an essential property of a triangle: if it ceases have three sides, it is no longer a triangle. Essential properties allow for no exceptions, so if property P is essential to being an F, then anything without P would also not be an F.

Continuing the triangle example, the specific color of a triangle, say blue, is an accidental property. This is not because it became blue as the result of an accident involving paint, but because ceasing to be blue would not make it cease to be a triangle. As such, accidental properties allow for exceptions.

Making an inference from an essential property would not be an error. For example, inferring that a specific triangle has three sides because triangles necessarily have three sides would be good reasoning. Treating an accidental property as an essential property and making this sort of inference would be an error. For example, while the vast majority of mammals lack pouches, lacking a pouch is not an essential property of mammals. So to infer that a marsupial lacks a pouch because it is a mammal would involve this sort of error.

The fallacy can occur in cases literally involving rules (such as laws) or cases in which the rule is a bit more metaphorical (such as a rule of thumb).

Example #1
"According to the constitution, people have a right to privacy. John beat his wife in private, so to arrest him for that would violate his right to privacy. So, he should not be arrested."

Example #2
Jane: "Please stop posting lies about me in your blog."
Jim: "Like hell I will. I know my rights and I have a right to free expression!"
Jane: "Then I will have to sue you for libel."
Jim: "Go right ahead. You'll never win. Freedom of the press, babycakes. That means I am free to write whatever I want and there is nothing you can do."

Example #3
1. Birds fly.
2. Penguins are birds.
3. Therefore, penguins fly.

Ad Hominem

Also Known as: Ad Hominem Abusive, Personal Attack
Description:

Translated from Latin to English, "ad Hominem" means "to the man." Some people translate it as "against the man" while others prefer the gender neutral "to/against the person." But, a fallacy by any other name would still stink.

An ad Hominem is a general category of fallacies in which a claim or argument is rejected on the basis of some irrelevant fact about the author of or the person presenting the claim or argument. Typically, this fallacy involves two steps. First, an attack against the character of person making the claim, her circumstances, or her actions is made (or the character, circumstances, or actions of the person reporting the claim). Second, this attack is taken to be evidence against the claim or argument the person in question is making (or presenting). This type of "argument" has the following form:

1. Person A makes claim X.
2. Person B makes an attack on person A.
3. Therefore A's claim is false.

The reason why an ad Hominem (of any kind) is a fallacy is that the character, circumstances, or actions of a person do not (in most cases) have a bearing on the truth or falsity of the claim being made (or the quality of the argument being made).

Example#1:
Bill: "I believe that abortion is morally wrong."
Dave: "Of course you would say that, you're a priest."
Bill: "What about the arguments I gave to support my position?"
Dave: "Those don't count. Like I said, you're a priest, so you have to say that abortion is wrong. Further, you are just a lackey to the Pope, so I can't believe what you say."

Example#2:
John: "Sally was saying that people shouldn't hunt animals or kill them for food or clothing. She also…"
Wanda: "Well, Sally is a sissy crybaby who loves animals way too much."
John: "So?"
Wanda: "That means she is wrong about that animal stuff. Also, if we weren't supposed to eat 'em, they wouldn't be made of meat."

Ad Hominem Tu Quoque

Also Known as: "You Too Fallacy"
Description:
This fallacy is committed when it is concluded that a person's claim is false because 1) it is inconsistent with something else a person has said or 2) what a person says is inconsistent with her actions. This type of "argument" has the following form:

1. Person A makes claim X.
2. Person B asserts that A's actions or past claims are inconsistent with the truth of claim X.
3. Therefore X is false.

The fact that a person makes inconsistent claims does not make any particular claim he makes false (although of any pair of inconsistent claims only one can be true—but both can be false). Also, the fact that a person's claims are not consistent with his actions might indicate that the person is a hypocrite but this does not prove his claims are false.

Example #1:
Bill: "Smoking is very unhealthy and leads to all sorts of problems. So take my advice and never start."
Jill: "Well, I certainly don't want to get cancer."
Bill: "I'm going to get a smoke. Want to join me Dave?"
Jill: "Well, I guess smoking can't be that bad. After all, Bill smokes."

Example #2:
Jill: "I think the gun control bill shouldn't be supported because it won't be effective and will waste money."
Bill: "Well, just last month you supported the bill. So I guess you're wrong now."

Example #3:
Peter: "Based on the arguments I have presented, it is evident that it is morally wrong to use animals for food or clothing."
Bill: "But you are wearing a leather jacket and you have a roast beef sandwich in your hand! How can you say that using animals for food and clothing is wrong!"

Amphiboly, Fallacy of

Description:
This fallacy occurs when a conclusion is drawn from a premise or premises that are ambiguous due to their grammatical structure. This fallacy has the following form:

1. Grammatically ambiguous premises are presented.
2. Conclusion C is drawn from these premises.

Amphiboly is a specific type of ambiguity caused by grammatical structure. Briefly put, something is ambiguous when it has two or more meanings and the context does not make it clear which is intended. Some texts refer to amphiboly as syntactical ambiguity (as contrasted with semantic ambiguity). This sort of ambiguity is often funny, as in the classic Groucho Marx line: "one morning I shot an elephant in my pajamas. How he got into my pajamas I'll never know."

Ambiguity is not itself a fallacy, but rather a lack of clarity in language (which might be intentional or accidental). The fallacy of amphiboly occurs when an inference is drawn from a premise or premises on the basis of such a grammatical ambiguity.

While this fallacy is not particularly common, it is somewhat famous thanks to King Croesus of Lydia, as shown in the following example. This example illustrates how a person can fall prey to the fallacy by drawing the conclusion he favors from premise that is ambiguous. While Croesus destroyed an empire, it was his own.

Example #1
King Croesus: "Oracle, if I go to war with Cyrus the King of Persia, then what will happen?"
Oracle of Delphi: "If Croesus went to war with Cyrus he would destroy a mighty kingdom."
King Croesus: "Excellent! After I destroy Cyrus, I shall make many and generous offerings to the gods."

Example #2
Roger: "Janet told Sally that she had made an error."
Ted: "Wow, I'm impressed that Janet was willing to admit the error she made."

Example #3
Lawyer: "Richard Jones left $20,000 and his cat, Mr. Whiskerpants, to Sally Jones and Daniel Jones."
Sally: "Looks like I get the money and you get that darn cat."
Daniel: "What?"
Mr. Whiskerpants: "Meow."

Anecdotal Evidence, Fallacy Of

Also Known as: Appeal to Anecdote
Description: This fallacy is committed when a person draws a conclusion about a population based on an anecdote (a story) about one or a very small number of cases. The fallacy is also committed when someone rejects reasonable statistical data supporting a claim in favor of a single example or small number of examples that go against the claim. The fallacy is considered by some to be a variation on hasty generalization. It has the following forms:

Form One
1. Anecdote A is told about a member (or small number of members) of Population P.
2. Conclusion C is drawn about Population P based on Anecdote A.

Form Two
1. Reasonable statistical evidence S exists for general claim C.
2. Anecdote A is presented that is an exception to or goes against general claim C.
3. Conclusion: General claim C is rejected.

This fallacy is similar to hasty generalization and a similar sort of error is committed, namely drawing an inference based on a sample that is inadequate in size relative to the conclusion. The main difference between hasty generalization and anecdotal evidence is that the fallacy anecdotal evidence involves using a story (anecdote) as the sample.

People often fall victim to this fallacy because stories and anecdotes tend to have more psychological influence than statistical data. This leads people to infer that what is true in an anecdote must be true of the whole population or that an anecdote justifies rejecting statistical evidence in favor of said anecdote. Not surprisingly, people most commonly accept this fallacy because they would prefer that what is true in the anecdote is true for the whole population. For example, a person who smokes might try to convince herself that smoking will not hurt her because her Aunt Jane smoked 52 cigars a day and lived until she was 104.

As the example suggests, this sort of poor reasoning can be used in the context of causal reasoning. In addition to cases involving individual causation (such as Jane not getting cancer) this poor reasoning is commonly applied to causal claims about populations. What typically occurs is that a person rejects a general causal claim such as smoking causes cancer in favor of an anecdote in which a person smoked but did not get cancer. While this anecdote does show that it is not true that all people who smoke get cancer, it does not prove that smoking does not cause cancer. This is because establishing that C is a causal factor for effect E in population P is a matter of showing that there would be more cases of E if all members of P were exposed to C than if none were. Showing that there are some anecdotal cases in which members of P were exposed to C but did not show effect E does not show that C does not cause E.

Naturally, the exceptions given in the anecdotes can provide a reason to be suspicious of the alleged causal connection but this suspicion must be proportional to the evidence provided by the anecdote. For example, the fact that Alan Magee survived a fall of 20,000 feet from his B-17 bomber in WWII does show that a human can survive such a fall. However, it does not serve to disprove the general claim that falls from great heights are generally fatal.

Anecdotes can also provide the basis for additional research. For example, the fact that some people are able to be exposed to certain pathogens without getting sick suggests that they would be well worth examining to see how their immunity works and whether or not this could benefit the general population. As another example, the fact that people do survive falls from aircraft does provide a reason for investigating how this works and how this might be useful.

Example #1
Jane: "Uncle Bill smoked a pack a day since he was 11 and he lived to be 90. So all that talk about smoking being bad is just a bunch of garbage."

Example #2
John: "Oh no! That woman is bringing pit bull into the dog park! Everyone grab their dogs and get out!"
Sally: "Oh, don't worry. I know that people think that pit bulls are aggressive and that there are all these statistics about them being dangerous dogs."
John: "Yeah, that is why I'm leaving before your monster kills my dog."
Sally: "But look at how sweet my pit bull Lady Buttercup is—she has never hurt anyone. So, all that bull about pit bulls being aggressive is just that: bull."

Example #3
Bill: "Hey Sally, you look a bit under the weather."
Sally: "Yeah, I think I'm getting a cold. In the summer. In Florida. That sucks."
Bill: "My dad and I almost never get colds. You should do what we do."
Sally: "What is that?"
Bill: "Drink red wine with every meal. My dad said that is the secret to avoiding colds. When I got old enough to buy wine, I started doing it."
Sally: "Every meal? Even breakfast?"
Bill: "Yes."
Sally: "Red wine goes with donuts?"
Bill: "Yes."
Ted: "That is baloney. I know a guy who did that and he had colds all the time. Now, this other guy told me that having a slice of cheese with every meal keeps the colds away. I never saw him so much as sniffle."
Sally: "Why not just have wine and cheese every meal?"

Example #4

Fred: "You are wasting time studying."

George: "What? Why aren't you studying? The test is going to be really hard."

Fred: "No need."

George: "You're not going to cheat are you?"

Fred: "No, of course not! But I heard about this woman, Keisha. She aced the last test and went to the movies and forgot to study. So, I'm going with the Keisha Method—I just need to pick a movie."

Appeal to the Consequences of a Belief

Description:

The Appeal to the Consequences of a Belief is a fallacy that comes in the following patterns:

#1: X is true because if people did not accept X as being true, then there would be negative consequences.

#2: X is false because if people did not accept X as being false, then there would be negative consequences.

#3: X is true because accepting that X is true has positive consequences.

#4: X is false because accepting that X is false has positive consequences.

#5: I wish that X were true, therefore X is true. This is known as Wishful Thinking.

#6: I wish that X were false, therefore X is false. This is known as Wishful Thinking.

This line of "reasoning" is fallacious because the consequences of a belief have no bearing on whether the belief is true or false. For example, if someone were to say "If sixteen-headed purple unicorns don't exist, then I would be miserable, so they must exist", it would be clear that this would not be a good line of reasoning. It is important to note that the consequences in question are the consequences that stem from the belief. It is important to distinguish between a rational reason to believe (RRB) (evidence) and a prudential reason to believe (PRB) (motivation). A RRB is evidence that objectively and logically supports the claim. A PRB is a reason to accept the belief because of some external factor (such as fear, a threat, or a benefit or harm that may stem from the belief) that is relevant to what a person values but is not relevant to the truth or falsity of the claim.

The nature of the fallacy is especially clear in the case of Wishful thinking. Obviously, merely wishing that something is true does not make it true. This fallacy differs from the Appeal to Belief fallacy in that the Appeal to Belief involves taking a claim that most people believe that X is true to be evidence for X being true.

Example #1:
God must exist! If God did not exist, then all basis for morality would be lost and the world would be a horrible place!

Example #2:
It can never happen to me. If I believed it could, I could never sleep soundly at night.

Example #3:
I don't think that there will be a nuclear war. If I believed that, I wouldn't be able to get up in the morning. I mean, how depressing.

Example #4:
I acknowledge that I have no argument for the existence of God. However, I have a great desire for God to exist and for there to be an afterlife. Therefore I accept that God exists.

Appeal to Authority, Fallacious

Also Known as: Misuse of Authority, Irrelevant Authority, Questionable Authority, Inappropriate Authority, Ad Verecundiam
Description:
A fallacious appeal to Authority is a fallacy with the following form:

1. Person A is (claimed to be) an authority on subject S.
2. Person A makes claim C about subject S.
3. Therefore, C is true.

This reasoning is fallacious when the person in question is not a legitimate authority on the subject. More formally, if person A is not qualified to make reliable claims in subject S, then the argument will be fallacious.

In such cases the reasoning is flawed because the fact that an unqualified person makes a claim does not provide any justification for the claim. The claim could be true, but the fact that an unqualified person made the claim does not provide any rational reason to accept the claim as true.

When a person falls prey to this fallacy, they are accepting a claim as true without there being adequate evidence to do so. More specifically, the person is accepting the claim because they erroneously believe that the person making the claim is a legitimate expert and hence that the claim is reasonable to accept. Since people have a tendency to believe authorities (and there are, in fact, good reasons to accept some claims made by authorities) this fallacy is a fairly common one.

Since this sort of reasoning is fallacious only when the person is not a legitimate authority in a particular context, it is necessary to provide some acceptable standards of assessment. The following standards are widely accepted:

1. The person has sufficient expertise in the subject matter in question.
Claims made by a person who lacks the needed degree of expertise to make a reliable claim will, obviously, not be well supported. In contrast, claims made by a person with the needed degree of expertise will be supported by the person's reliability in the area.

Determining whether or not a person has the needed degree of expertise can often be very difficult. In academic fields (such as philosophy, engineering, history, etc.), the person's formal education, academic performance, publications, membership in professional societies, papers presented, awards won and so forth can all be reliable indicators of expertise. Outside of academic fields, other standards will apply. For example, having sufficient expertise to make a reliable claim about how to tie a shoe lace only requires the ability to tie the shoe lace and impart that information to others. It should be noted that being an expert does not always require having a university degree. Many people have high degrees of expertise in sophisticated subjects without having ever attended a university. Further, it should not be simply assumed that a person with a degree is an expert.

Of course, what is required to be an expert is often a matter of great debate. For example, some people have (and do) claim expertise in certain (even all) areas because of a divine inspiration or a special gift. The followers of such people accept such credentials as establishing the person's expertise while others often see these self-proclaimed experts as deluded or even as charlatans. In other situations, people debate over what sort of education and experience is needed to be an expert. Thus, what one person may take to be a fallacious appeal another person might take to be a well-supported line of reasoning. Fortunately, many cases do not involve such debate.

2. The claim being made by the person is within her area(s) of expertise.

If a person makes a claim about some subject outside of his area(s) of expertise, then the person is not an expert in that context. Hence, the claim in question is not backed by the required degree of expertise and is not reliable.

It is very important to remember that because of the vast scope of human knowledge and skill it is simply not possible for one person to be an expert on everything. Hence, experts will only be true experts in respect to certain subject areas. In most other areas they will have little or no expertise. Thus, it is important to determine what subject area a claim falls under.

It is also very important to note that expertise in one area does not automatically confer expertise in another. For example, being an expert physicist does not automatically make a person an expert on morality or politics. Unfortunately, this is often overlooked or intentionally ignored. In fact, a great deal of advertising rests on a violation of this condition. As anyone who watches television knows, it is extremely common to get famous actors and sports heroes to endorse products that they are not qualified to assess. For example, a person may be a great actor, but that does not automatically make him an expert on cars or shaving or underwear or diets or politics.

3. There is an adequate degree of agreement among the other experts in the subject in question.

If there is a significant amount of legitimate dispute among the experts within a subject, then it will fallacious to make an Appeal to Authority using the disputing experts. This is because for almost any claim being made and "supported" by one expert there will be a counterclaim that is made and "supported" by another expert. In such cases an Appeal to Authority would tend to be futile. In such cases, the dispute has to be settled by consideration of the actual issues under dispute. Since either side in such a dispute can invoke experts, the dispute cannot be rationally settled by Appeals to Authority.

There are many fields in which there is a significant amount of legitimate dispute. Economics is a good example of such a disputed field. Anyone who is familiar with economics knows that there are many plausible theories that are incompatible with one another. Because of this, one expert economist could sincerely claim that the deficit is the key factor while another equally qualified individual could assert the exact opposite. Another area where dispute is very common (and well known) is in the area of psychology and psychiatry. As has been demonstrated in various trials, it is possible to find one expert that will assert that an individual is insane and not competent to stand trial and to find another equally qualified expert who will testify, under oath, that the same individual is both sane and competent to stand trial. Obviously, one cannot rely on an Appeal to Authority in such a situation without making a fallacious argument. Such an argument would be fallacious since the evidence would not warrant accepting the conclusion.

It is important to keep in mind that no field has complete agreement, so some degree of dispute is acceptable. How much is acceptable is, of course, a matter of serious debate. It is also important to keep in mind that even a field with a great deal of internal dispute might contain areas of significant agreement. In such cases, an Appeal to Authority could be legitimate.

4. The person in question is not significantly biased.

If an expert is significantly biased then the claims he makes within his are of bias will be less reliable. Since a biased expert will not be reliable, an Argument from Authority based on a biased expert will be fallacious. This is because the evidence will not justify accepting the claim.

Experts, being people, are vulnerable to biases and prejudices. If there is evidence that a person is biased in some manner that would affect the reliability of her claims, then an Argument from Authority based on that person is likely to be fallacious. Even if the claim is actually true, the fact that the expert is biased weakens the argument. This is because there would be reason to believe that the expert might not be making the claim because he has carefully considered it using his expertise. Rather, there would be reason to believe that the claim is being made because of the expert's bias or prejudice.

It is important to remember that no person is completely objective. At the very least, a person will be favorable towards her own views (otherwise she would probably not hold them). Because of this, some degree of bias must be accepted, provided that the bias is not significant. What counts as a significant degree of bias is open to dispute and can vary a great deal from case to case. For example, many people would probably suspect that doctors who were paid by tobacco companies to research the effects of smoking would be biased while other people might believe (or claim) that they would be able to remain objective.

5. The area of expertise is a legitimate area or discipline.

Certain areas in which a person may claim expertise may have no legitimacy or validity as areas of knowledge or study. Obviously, claims made in such areas will not be very reliable.

What counts as a legitimate area of expertise is sometimes difficult to determine. However, there are cases which are fairly clear cut. For example, if a person claimed to be an expert at something he called "chromabullet therapy" and asserted that firing painted rifle bullets at a person would cure cancer it would not be very reasonable to accept his claim based on his "expertise." After all, his expertise is in an area which is devoid of legitimate content. The general idea is that to be a legitimate expert a person must have mastery over a real field or area of knowledge.

As noted above, determining the legitimacy of a field can often be difficult. In European history, various scientists had to struggle with the Church and established traditions to establish the validity of their disciplines. For example, experts on evolution faced an uphill battle in getting the legitimacy of their area accepted.

A modern example involves psychic phenomenon. Some people claim that they are certified "master psychics" and that they are actually experts in the field. Other people contend that their claims of being certified "master psychics" are simply absurd since there is no real content to such an area of expertise. If these people are right, then anyone who accepts the claims of these "master psychics" as true are victims of a fallacious appeal to authority.

6. The authority in question must be identified.

A common variation of the typical Appeal to Authority fallacy is an Appeal to an Unnamed Authority. This fallacy is Also Known as an Appeal to an Unidentified Authority.

This fallacy is committed when a person asserts that a claim is true because an expert or authority makes the claim and the person does not actually identify the expert. Since the expert is not named or identified, there is no way to tell if the person is actually an expert. Unless the person is identified and has his expertise established, there is no reason to accept the claim.

This sort of reasoning is not unusual. Typically, the person making the argument will say things like "I have a book that says...", or "they say...", or "the experts say...", or "scientists believe that...", or "I read in the paper.." or "I saw on TV..." or some similar statement. in such cases the person is often hoping that the listener(s) will simply accept the unidentified source as a legitimate authority and believe the claim being made. If a person accepts the claim simply because they accept the unidentified source as an expert (without good reason to do so), he has fallen prey to this fallacy.

Non-Fallacious Appeals to Authority

As suggested above, not all Appeals to Authority are fallacious. This is fortunate since people have to rely on experts. This is because no one person can be an expert on everything and people do not have the time or ability to investigate every single claim themselves.

In many cases, Arguments from Authority will be good arguments. For example, when a person goes to a skilled doctor and the doctor tells him that he has a cold, then the patient has good reason to accept the doctor's conclusion. As another example, if a person's computer is acting odd and his friend, who is a computer expert, tells him it is probably his hard drive then he has good reason to believe her.

What distinguishes a fallacious Appeal to Authority from a good Appeal to Authority is that the argument meets the six conditions discussed above.

In a good Appeal to Authority, there is reason to believe the claim because the expert says the claim is true. This is because a person who is a legitimate expert is more likely to be right than wrong when making considered claims within her area of expertise. In a sense, the claim is being accepted because it is reasonable to believe that the expert has tested the claim and found it to be reliable. So, if the expert has found it to be reliable, then it is reasonable to accept it as being true. Thus, the listener is accepting a claim based on the testimony of the expert.

It should be noted that even a good Appeal to Authority is not an exceptionally strong argument. After all, in such cases a claim is being accepted as true simply because a person is asserting that it is true. The person may be an expert, but her expertise does not really bear on the truth of the claim. This is because the expertise of a person does not actually determine whether the claim is true or false. Hence, arguments that deal directly with evidence relating to the claim itself will tend to be stronger.

Example #1:
Bill and Jane are arguing about the morality of abortion:

Bill: "I believe that abortion is morally acceptable. After all, a woman should have a right to her own body."
Jane: 'I disagree completely. Dr. Johan Skarn says that abortion is always morally wrong, regardless of the situation. He has to be right, after all, he is a respected expert in his field."
Bill: "I've never heard of Dr. Skarn. Who is he?"
Jane: "He's the guy that won the Nobel Prize in physics for his work on cold fusion."
Bill: "I see. Does he have any expertise in morality or ethics?"
Jane: "I don't know. But he's a world famous expert, so I believe him."

Example #2:
Dave and Kintaro are arguing about Stalin's reign in the Soviet Union. Dave has

been arguing that Stalin was a great leader while Kintaro disagrees with him.

Kintaro: "I don't see how you can consider Stalin to be a great leader. He killed millions of his own people, he crippled the Soviet economy, kept most of the people in fear and laid the foundations for the violence that is occurring in much of Eastern Europe."

Dave: "Yeah, well you say that. However, I have a book at home that says that Stalin was acting in the best interest of the people. The millions that were killed were vicious enemies of the state and they had to be killed to protect the rest of the peaceful citizens. This book lays it all out, so it has to be true."

Example #3:

I'm not a doctor, but I play one on the hit series "Bimbos and Studmuffins in the OR." You can take it from me that when you need a fast acting, effective and safe pain killer there is nothing better than MorphiDope 2000. That is my considered medical opinion.

Example #4:

Siphwe and Sasha are having a conversation:

Sasha: "I played the lottery today and I know I am going to win something."

Siphwe: "What did you do, rig the outcome?"

Sasha: "No, silly. I called my Super Psychic Buddy at the 1-900-MindPower number. After consulting his magic Californian Tarot deck, he told me my lucky numbers."

Siphwe: "And you believed him?"

Sasha: "Certainly, he is a certified Californian Master-Mind Psychic. That is why I believe what he has to say. I mean, like, who else would know what my lucky numbers are?"

Appeal to Belief

Description:

Appeal to Belief is a fallacy that has this general pattern:

1. Most people believe that a claim, X, is true.
2. Therefore X is true.

This line of "reasoning" is fallacious because the fact that many people believe a claim does not, in general, serve as evidence that the claim is true.

There are, however, some cases when the fact that many people accept a claim as true is an indication that it is true. For example, while you are visiting Maine, you are told by several people that they believe that people older than 16 need to buy a fishing license in order to fish. Barring reasons to doubt these people, their statements give you reason to believe that anyone over 16 will need to buy a fishing license.

There are also cases in which what people believe actually determines the truth of a claim. For example, the truth of claims about manners and proper behavior might simply depend on what people believe to be good manners and proper behavior. Another example is the case of community standards, which are often taken to be the standards that most people accept. In some cases, what violates certain community standards is taken to be obscene. In such cases, for the claim "x is obscene" to be true is for most people in that community to believe that x is obscene. In such cases it is still prudent to question the justification of the individual beliefs.

Example #1:
At one time, most people in Europe believed that the earth was the center of the solar system (at least most of those who had beliefs about such things). However, this belief turned out to be false.

Example #2:
God must exist. After all, I just saw a poll that says 85% of all Americans believe in God.

Example #3:
Of course there is nothing wrong with drinking. Ask anyone, he'll tell you that he thinks drinking is just fine.

Appeal to Common Practice

Description:
The Appeal to Common Practice is a fallacy with the following structure:

1. X is a common action.
2. Therefore X is correct/moral/justified/reasonable, etc.

The basic idea behind the fallacy is that the fact that most people do X is used as "evidence" to support the action or practice. It is a fallacy because the mere fact that most people do something does not make it correct, moral, justified, or reasonable.

An appeal to fair play, which might seem to be an appeal to common practice, need not be a fallacy. For example, a woman working in an office might say "the men who do the same job as me get paid more than I do, so it would be right for me to get paid the same as them." This would not be a fallacy as long as there was no relevant difference between her and the men (in terms of ability, experience, hours worked, etc.). More formally:

1. It is common practice to treat people of type Y in manner X and to treat people of type Z in a different manner.
2. There is no relevant difference between people of type Y and type Z.
3. Therefore people of type Z should be treated in manner X, too.

This argument rests heavily on the principle of relevant difference. On this principle two people, A and B, can only be treated differently if and only if there is a relevant difference between them. For example, it would be fine for me to give a better grade to A than B if A did better work than B. However, it would be wrong of me to give A a better grade than B simply because A has red hair and B has blonde hair.

There might be some cases in which the fact that most people accept X as moral entails that X is moral. For example, one view of morality is that morality is relative to the practices of a culture, time, person, etc. If what is moral is determined by what is commonly practiced, then this argument:

1. Most people do X.
2. Therefore X is morally correct.

would not be a fallacy. This would however entail some odd results. For example, imagine that there are only 100 people on earth. 60 of them do not steal or cheat and 40 do. At this time, stealing and cheating would be wrong. The next day, a natural disaster kills 30 of the 60 people who do not cheat or steal. Now it is morally correct to cheat and steal. Thus, it would be possible to change the moral order of the world to one's view simply by eliminating those who disagree.

Example #1:
Director Jones is in charge of running a state waste management program. When it is found that the program is rife with corruption, Jones says "This program has its problems, but nothing goes on in this program that doesn't go on in all state programs."

Example #2:
"Yeah, I know some people say that cheating on tests is wrong. But we all know that everyone does it, so it's okay."

Example #3:
"Sure, some people buy into that equality crap. However, we know that everyone pays women less than men. It's okay, too. Since everyone does it, it can't really be wrong."

Example #4:
"There is nothing wrong with requiring multicultural classes, even at the expense of core subjects. After all, all of the universities and colleges are pushing multiculturalism."

Appeal to Emotion

Description:
An Appeal to Emotion is a fallacy with the following structure:

1. Favorable emotions are associated with X.
2. Therefore, X is true.

This fallacy is committed when someone manipulates peoples' emotions in order to get them to accept a claim as being true. More formally, this sort of "reasoning" involves the substitution of various means of producing strong emotions in place of evidence for a claim. If the favorable emotions associated with X influence the person to accept X as true because they "feel good about X," then he has fallen prey to the fallacy.

This sort of "reasoning" is very common in politics and it serves as the basis for a large portion of modern advertising. Most political speeches are aimed at generating feelings in people so that these feelings will get them to vote or act a certain way. In the case of advertising, the commercials are aimed at evoking emotions that will influence people to buy certain products. In most cases, such speeches and commercials are notoriously free of real evidence.

This sort of "reasoning" is quite evidently fallacious. It is fallacious because using various tactics to incite emotions in people does not serve as evidence for a claim. For example, if a person were able to inspire in a person an incredible hatred of the claim that 1+1 = 2 and then inspired the person to love the claim that 1+1 =3, it would hardly follow that the claim that 1+1 = 3 would be adequately supported.

It should be noted that in many cases it is not particularly obvious that the person committing the fallacy is attempting to support a claim. In many cases, the user of the fallacy will appear to be attempting to move people to take an action, such as buying a product or fighting in a war. However, it is possible to determine what sort of claim the person is actually attempting to support. In such cases one needs to ask "what sort of claim is this person attempting to get people to accept and act on?" Determining this claim (or claims) might take some work. However, in many cases it will be quite evident. For example, if a political leader is attempting to convince her followers to participate in certain acts of violence by the use of a hate speech, then her claim would be "you should participate in these acts of violence." In this case, the "evidence" would be the hatred evoked in the followers. This hatred would serve to make them favorable inclined towards the claim that they should engage in the acts of violence. As another example, a beer commercial might show happy, scantily clad men and women prancing about a beach, guzzling beer. In this case the claim would be "you should buy this beer." The "evidence" would be the excitement evoked by seeing the beautiful people guzzling the beer.

This fallacy is actually an extremely effective persuasive device. As many people have argued, peoples' emotions often carry much more force than their reason. Logical argumentation is often difficult and time consuming and it rarely has the power to spur people to action. It is the power of this fallacy that explains its great popularity and wide usage. However, it is still a fallacy.

In all fairness it must be noted that the use of tactics to inspire emotions is an important skill. Without an appeal to peoples' emotions, it is often difficult to get them to take action or to perform at their best. For example, no good coach presents her team with syllogisms before the big game. Instead she inspires them with emotional terms and attempts to "fire" them up. There is nothing inherently wrong with this. However, it is not any acceptable form of argumentation. As long as one is able to clearly distinguish between what inspires emotions and what justifies a claim, one is unlikely to fall prey to this fallacy.

As a final point, in many cases it will be difficult to distinguish an Appeal to Emotion from some other fallacies and in many cases multiple fallacies may be committed. For example, many Ad Hominems will be very similar to Appeals to Emotion and, in some cases, both fallacies will be committed. As an example, a leader might attempt to invoke hatred of a person to inspire his followers to accept that they should reject her claims. The same attack could function as an Appeal to Emotion and a Personal Attack. In the first case, the attack would be aimed at making the followers feel very favorable about rejecting her claims. In the second case, the attack would be aimed at making the followers reject the person's claims because of some perceived (or imagined) defect in her character.

This fallacy is related to the Appeal to Popularity fallacy. Despite the differences between these two fallacies, they are both united by the fact that they involve appeals to emotions. In both cases the fallacies aim at getting people to accept claims based on how they or others feel about the claims and not based on evidence for the claims.

Another way to look at these two fallacies is as follows

Appeal to Popularity
1. Most people approve of X.
2. So, I should approve of X, too.
3. Since I approve of X, X must be true.

Appeal to Emotion
1. I approve of X.
2. Therefore, X is true.

On this view, in an Appeal to Popularity the claim is accepted because most people approve of the claim. In the case of an Appeal to Emotion the claim is accepted because the individual approves of the claim because of the emotion of approval he feels in regards to the claim.

Example #1:
The new PowerTangerine computer gives you the power you need. If you buy one, people will envy your power. They will look up to you and wish they were just like you. You will know the true joy of power. TangerinePower.

Example #2:
The new UltraSkinny diet will make you feel great. No longer be troubled by your weight. Enjoy the admiring stares of the opposite sex. Revel in your new freedom from fat. You will know true happiness if you try our diet!

Example #3:
Bill goes to hear a politician speak. The politician tells the crowd about the evils of the government and the need to throw out the people who are currently in office. After hearing the speech, Bill is full of hatred for the current politicians. Because of this, he feels good about getting rid of the old politicians and accepts that it is the right thing to do because of how he feels.

Appeal to Envy

Description:

This fallacy occurs when a person infers a fault in another based on the emotion of envy. The fallacy has the following form:

1. Person A feels envious of person B.
2. Therefore person B has fault F.

This sort of "reasoning" is fallacious because a feeling of envy does not prove that a person has a fault or flaw. This error is tempting because people are often inclined to think badly of those they envy.

Naturally, while envy is generally regarded as a negative emotion, the feeling of envy is not a fallacy.

Example #1

"Sure he is rich and handsome, but I'm sure he doesn't have any friends."

Example #2

Sally: "You know rich people are very unhappy."
Ted: "Why think that? After all, they can solve many problems with money."
Sally: "I just know they are. I mean, look at their amazing lives: wealth, luxury goods, trips, beautiful boyfriends, and awesomeness. They just have to be unhappy. They just do."

Appeal to Fear

Also Known as: Scare Tactics, Appeal to Force, Ad Baculum
Description:

The Appeal to Fear is a fallacy with the following pattern:

1. Y is presented (a claim that is intended to produce fear).
2. Therefore claim X is true (a claim that is generally, but need not be, related to Y in some manner).

This line of "reasoning" is fallacious because creating fear in people does not constitute evidence for a claim.

It is important to distinguish between a rational reason to believe (RRB) (evidence) and a prudential reason to believe (PRB) (motivation). A RRB is evidence that objectively and logically supports the claim. A PRB is a reason to accept the belief because of some external factor (such as fear, a threat, or a benefit or harm that may stem from the belief) that is relevant to what a person values but is not relevant to the truth or falsity of the claim. For example, it might be prudent to not fail the son of your department chairperson because you fear he will make life tough for you. However, this does not provide evidence for the claim that the son deserves to pass the class.

Example #1:
You know, Professor Smith, I really need to get an A in this class. I'd like to stop by during your office hours later to discuss my grade. I'll be in your building anyways, visiting my father. He's your dean, by the way. I'll see you later.

Example #2:
I don't think a Red Ryder BB rifle would make a good present for you. They are very dangerous and you'll put your eye out. Now, don't you agree that you should think of another gift idea?

Example #3:
You must believe that God exists. After all, if you do not accept the existence of God, then you will face the horrors of hell.

Example #4:
You shouldn't say such things against multiculturalism! If the chair heard what you were saying, you would never receive tenure. So, you had just better learn to accept that it is simply wrong to speak out against it.

Appeal to Flattery

Also known as: Apple Polishing, various "colorful" expressions
Description:
An Appeal to Flattery is a fallacy of the following form:

1. Person A is flattered by person B.
2. Person B makes claim X.
3. Therefore X is true.

The basic idea behind this fallacy is that flattery is presented in the place of evidence for accepting a claim. This sort of "reasoning" is fallacious because flattery is not, in fact, evidence for a claim. This is especially clear in a case like this: "My Bill, that is a really nice tie. By the way, it is quite clear that 1+1=43."

Example #1:
Might I say that this is the best philosophy class I've ever taken. By the way, about those two points I need to get an A...

Example #2:
That was a wonderful joke about AIDS boss, and I agree with you that the damn liberals are wrecking the country. Now about my raise...

Example #3:
That was a singularly brilliant idea. I have never seen such a clear and eloquent defense of Plato's position. If you do not mind, I'll base my paper on it. Provided that you allow me a little extra time past the deadline to work on it.

Appeal to Group Identity

Also Known As: Group think fallacy
Description:

This fallacy occurs when an appeal to group identity is offered as a substitute for evidence for a claim. It has the following form:

1. An appeal, A, is made to a person or persons' identity with group G.
2. Therefore, claim C is true.

While the specific nature of the appeal can vary, the most common method of appealing to group identity involves an attempt to make use of the pride the group members feel regarding the specific group. While feeling pride and identifying with a group are not fallacious, to accept a claim based on group pride or identity would be an error. This is because feelings of pride and a feeling of group identity do not serve as evidence for a claim. A person can make this appeal to others or can make such an appeal to himself.

This fallacy can be used with any sort of group identity, such a political groups, ethnic groups, religious groups, and so on. One rather common version makes use of nationalism (pride in one's country) when attempting to get people to accept a claim (or accept that they should reject a claim). People can convince themselves that a claim is true (or false) based on their feeling of group identity or pride. As such, this fallacy can be self-inflicted.

That group identity does not serve as proof is easily shown by the following example: "I am proud of being a Flat-Earther, therefore the earth is flat."

This fallacy is easy to confuse with peer pressure, appeal to belief, and common practice. However, the mistake being made is different. While the peer pressure fallacy does involve a group, the mistake being made is that a claim is accepted based on fear of rejection by the group rather than because of pride in that group. In the case of appeal to belief, the error being made is that a claim is accepted on the basis that many people believe the claim. Common practice, as the name indicates, involves accepting that a practice is correct/good because it is common, rather than on the basis of identifying with a group that engages in that practice. People can commit multiple fallacies, so someone might appeal to group identity while also appealing to belief and to common practice.

Example #1

"Your blog post is truly awful. Your criticism of America's Middle East policy shows that you are not a real American. Me, I love America and I am proud to be an American. Since you obviously do not love America or have any pride in her greatness, you should pack up and move to Iran. I think this takes care of your criticisms."

Example #2

Fred: "America is responsible for global warming."

Sally: "Well, we do contribute more than our fair share to the problem."

Fred: "No, it is not just that Americans contribute more. American corporations and the American politicians set the world agenda and thus America is to blame for global warming."

Sally: "That seems a bit much. Surely other nations contribute as well. Look at China, for example. China is hardly an American puppet and they are cranking out cars and coal plants."

Fred: "You just don't get it. America is the cause of the world's problems."

Sally: "Wait; are you one of those 'blame America first' people?"

Fred: "That phrase is loaded, but I am proud to be on the left. We are the vanguard against America's misdeeds and will make the world a better place. I know we are right because I can feel it in my heart."

Sally: "So, you know you are right because you are proud of your elite group?"

Fred: "Yes. Maybe someday you will join us."

Sally: "Will I have to buy a Prius and an iPad?"

Fred: "Of course."

Example #3

"Sure, there are people who criticize the government. But, as the guy said, 'my country, wrong or right.' So, those critics need to shut up and accept that they are wrong. Or maybe someone should shut them up with some Second Amendment remedies."

Example #4

"I've seen a lot of debate about faith, but I know that my faith is the correct one. Every time that I think of my relation with God and my fellow believers, my heart swells with pride at our true and pure faith. I cannot help but feel sorry for those who blindly refuse to accept what we thus know to be true, but perhaps they will realize the foolishness of their error before it is too late."

Example #5

George: "Wow, that Mal Mart seems pretty bad. Lawsuits from women and minorities and so on, that shows they have some real problems going on."
Gerald: "You shut your Twinkie hole! I work at Mal Mart and I won't listen to you say anything bad about us!"
George: "Easy, I'm not attacking you!"
Gerald: "When you attack Mal Mart, you attack me. Now admit you are wrong!"
George: "What, just because you work there and think you are part of the big Mal Mart family? That has nothing to do with me being right or wrong about the company."
Gerald: "Shut up or I'll lower your prices."
George: "What?"

Appeal to Guilt

Also Known As: Guilt trip

An appeal to guilt is a fallacy in which a person substitutes a claim intended to create guilt for evidence in an argument. The form of the "argument" is as follows:

1. G is presented, with the intent to create a feeling of guilt in person P.
2. Therefore claim C is true.

This line of "reasoning" is fallacious because a feeling of guilt does not serve as evidence for a claim. The emotion of guilt, like all emotions, is not itself fallacious. However, to accept a claim as true based on the "evidence" of feeling guilt would be an error.

This fallacy is often used in an attempt to get a person to do something (to accept a claim that they should do something as being true) by trying to invoke a feeling of guilt. While it is appropriate to feel guilt when one has done something wrong, the fact that a person has been caused to feel guilty does not show that the person should feel guilty. The question of when a person should or should not feel guilt is primarily a matter for ethics rather than logic, which takes it beyond the intended scope of this book.

There are cases in which claims that logically serve as evidence can also evoke a feeling of guilt. In these cases, the feeling of guilt is still not evidence. The following shows a situation in which a person would probably feel guilt but in which there is also legitimate evidence for the claim being made:

Jane: "You really should help Sally move."
Hilda: "Moving is a drag. Besides, the game is on then."
Jane: "Sally helped you move. In fact, she spent all day helping you because no one else would."
Hilda: "Are you trying to guilt me into helping her?"
Jane: "Yeah, a bit. But you owe her. She helped you move and you really should feel bad if you don't lend her a hand."
Hilda: "She'll be fine. A lot of her friends are helping her out."
Jane: "And they are helping her because she helped them. That is what friends do. If you value her friendship, then you should go with me."

The above example does not involve a fallacy. While Jane does hope that Hilda will feel guilt and be motivated to help Sally, the fact that Sally helped Hilda does provide a legitimate reason as to why Hilda should help her. Naturally, it could be argued that helping people does not create a debt, but this would be a matter of substantial moral dispute rather than proof that Jane has made a logical error.

Example #1
Child: "I'm full."
Parent: "You need to finish all your food. There are children starving in Africa."
Child: "But broccoli is awful!"
Parent: "Those kids in Africa would love to have even a single piece of broccoli. Shame on you for not eating it."
Child: "Okay, I'll send them this broccoli!"
Parent: "No, you'll eat it."
Child: "But how does that help the starving kids?"
Parent: "Finish the broccoli!"

Example #2

Eric: "I need an iPad!"

Mother: "Don't you already have one?"

Eric: "That was the old iPad. I need a new iPad."

Mother: "You barely use the iPad you have now."

Eric: "If you love me, you'll get me one!"

Mother: "I don't think you need a new one now."

Eric: "How can you treat me like this? What sort of mother would let her son go to school without the latest iPad? You hate me!"

Mother: "Okay, I'll get you one."

Eric: "I need a new iPhone, too."

Mother: "I just bought you one!"

Eric: "The new one is a different color. That changes everything."

Mother: "Fine."

Example #3

Bill: "You're late. I planned dinner for when you were supposed to get home, so yours is cold now."

Kelly: "I'm sorry. The meeting ran a little longer than I expected. But the boss had good news for me—I got a raise!"

Bill: "Oh sure, show up late for dinner and throw a raise in my face, now that I'm not working!"

Kelly: "I didn't throw it in your face, I just…"

Bill: "You're robbing me of my manhood!"

Kelly: "I'm sorry!"

Bill: "Well, you can make it up to me by buying me a motorcycle."

Kelly: "Okay. I'm sorry about dinner and getting a raise."

Bill: "That's okay. You can use the raise to get me a really good motorcycle."

Appeal to Novelty

Also Known as: Appeal to the New, Newer is Better, Novelty

Description:

Appeal to Novelty is a fallacy that occurs when it is assumed that something is better or correct simply because it is new. This sort of "reasoning" has the following form:

1. X is new.

2. Therefore X is correct or better.

This sort of "reasoning" is fallacious because the novelty or newness of something does not automatically make it correct or better than something older. This is made quite obvious by the following example: Joe has proposed that 1+1 should now be equal to 3. When asked why people should accept this, he says that he just came up with the idea. Since it is newer than the idea that 1+1=2, it must be better.

This sort of "reasoning" is appealing for many reasons. First, "western culture" includes a very powerful commitment to the notion that new things must be better than old things. Second, the notion of progress (which seems to have come, in part, from the notion of evolution) implies that newer things will be superior to older things. Third, media advertising often sends the message that newer must be better. Because of these three factors (and others) people often accept that a new thing (idea, product, concept, etc.) must be better because it is new. Hence, Novelty is a somewhat common fallacy, especially in advertising.

It should not be assumed that old things must be better than new things (see the fallacy Appeal to Tradition) any more than it should be assumed that new things are better than old things. The age of a thing does not, in general, have any bearing on its quality or correctness (in this context).

Obviously, age does have a bearing in some contexts. For example, if a person concluded that his day old milk was better than his two-month old milk, he would not be committing an Appeal to Novelty. This is because in such cases the newness of the thing is relevant to its quality. Thus, the fallacy is committed only when the newness is not, in and of itself, relevant to the claim.

Example #1:
The Sadisike 900 pump-up glow shoe. It's better because it's new.

Example #2:
James: "So, what is this new plan?"
Biff: "Well, the latest thing in marketing techniques is the GK method. It is the latest thing out of the think tank. It is so new that the ink on the reports is still drying."
James: "Well, our old marketing method has been quite effective. I don't like the idea of jumping to a new method without a good reason."
Biff: "Well, we know that we have to stay on the cutting edge. That means new ideas and new techniques have to be used. The GK method is new, so it will do better than that old, dusty method."

Example #3:

Prof: "So you can see that a new and better morality is sweeping the nation. No longer are people with alternative lifestyles ashamed. No longer are people caught up in the outmoded moralities of the past."

Student: "Well, what about the ideas of the great thinkers of the past? Don't they have some valid points?"

Prof: "A good question. The answer is that they had some valid points in their own, barbaric times. But those are old, moldy moralities from a time long gone. Now is a time for new moralities. Progress and all that, you know."

Student: "So would you say that the new moralities are better because they are newer?"

Prof: "Exactly. Just as the dinosaurs died off to make way for new animals, the old ideas have to give way for the new ones. And just as humans are better than dinosaurs, the new ideas are better than the old. So newer is literally better."

Student: "I see."

Appeal to Pity

Also Known as: Ad Misericordiam

Description:

An Appeal to Pity is a fallacy in which a person substitutes a claim intended to create pity for evidence in an argument. The form of the "argument" is as follows:

1. P is presented, with the intent to create pity.
2. Therefore claim C is true.

This line of "reasoning" is fallacious because pity does not serve as evidence for a claim. This is extremely clear in the following case: "You must accept that 1+1=46, after all I'm dying…" While you may pity me because I am dying, it would hardly make my claim true.

This fallacy differs from the Appeal to the Consequences of a Belief (ACB). In the ACB fallacy, a person is using the effects of a belief as a substitute for evidence. In the Appeal to Pity, it is the feelings of pity or sympathy that are substituted for evidence.

It must be noted that there are cases in which claims that actually serve as evidence also evoke a feeling of pity. In such cases, the feeling of pity is still not evidence. The following is an example of a case in which a claim evokes pity and also serves as legitimate evidence:

Professor: "You missed the midterm, Bill."

Bill: "I know. I think you should let me take the makeup."

Professor: "Why?"

Bill: "I was hit by a truck on the way to the midterm. Since I had to go to the emergency room with a broken leg, I think I am entitled to a makeup."

Professor: "I'm sorry about the leg, Bill. Of course you can make it up."

The above example does not involve a fallacy. While the professor does feel sorry for Bill, she is justified in accepting Bill's claim that he deserves a makeup. After all getting run over by a truck would be a legitimate excuse for missing a test.

Example #1:
Jill: "He'd be a terrible coach for the team."

Bill: "He had his heart set on the job, and it would break if he didn't get it."

Jill: "Well, I guess he'll do an adequate job…"

Example #2:
"I'm positive that my work will meet your requirements. I really need the job since my grandmother is sick"

Example #3:
"I should receive an 'A' in this class. After all, if I don't get an 'A' I won't get the fellowship that I want."

Appeal to Popularity

Description:
The Appeal to Popularity has the following form:

1. Most people approve of X (have favorable emotions towards X).
2. Therefore X is true.

The basic idea is that a claim is accepted as being true simply because most people are favorably inclined towards the claim. More formally, the fact that most people have favorable emotions associated with the claim is substituted in place of actual evidence for the claim. A person falls prey to this fallacy if he accepts a claim as being true simply because most other people approve of the claim.

It is clearly fallacious to accept the approval of the majority as evidence for a claim. For example, suppose that a skilled speaker managed to get most people to absolutely love the claim that 1+1=3. It would still not be rational to accept this claim simply because most people approved of it. After all, mere approval is no substitute for a mathematical proof. At one time people approved of claims such as "the world is flat", "humans cannot survive at speeds greater than 25 miles per hour", "the sun revolves around the earth" but all these claims turned out to be false.

This sort of "reasoning" is quite common and can be quite an effective persuasive device. Since most humans tend to conform with the views of the majority, convincing a person that the majority approves of a claim is often an effective way to get him to accept it. Advertisers often use this tactic when they attempt to sell products by claiming that everyone uses and loves their products. In such cases they hope that people will accept the (purported) approval of others as a good reason to buy the product.

This fallacy is vaguely similar to such fallacies as Appeal to Belief and Appeal to Common Practice. However, in the case of an Ad Populum the appeal is to the fact that most people approve of a claim. In the case of an Appeal to Belief, the appeal is to the fact that most people believe a claim. In the case of an Appeal to Common Practice, the appeal is to the fact that many people take the action in question.

This fallacy is closely related to the Appeal to Emotion fallacy, as discussed in the entry for that fallacy.

Example #1:
My fellow Americans…there has been some talk that the government is overstepping its bounds by allowing police to enter people's homes without the warrants traditionally required by the Constitution. However, these are dangerous times and dangerous times require appropriate actions. I have in my office thousands of letters from people who let me know, in no uncertain terms, that they heartily endorse the war against terrorism in these United States. Because of this overwhelming approval, it is evident that the police are doing the right thing.

Example #2:
I read the other day that most people really like the new gun control laws. I was sort of suspicious of them, but I guess if most people like them, then they must be okay.

Example #3:
Jill and Jane have some concerns that the rules their sorority has set are racist in character. Since Jill is a decent person, she brings her concerns up in the next meeting. The president of the sorority assures her that there is nothing wrong with

the rules, since the majority of the sisters like them. Jane accepts this ruling but Jill decides to leave the sorority.

Appeal to Ridicule

Also Known as: Appeal to Mockery, The Horse Laugh.
Description:
The Appeal to Ridicule is a fallacy in which ridicule or mockery is substituted for evidence in an "argument." This line of "reasoning" has the following form:

1. X, which is some form of ridicule is presented (typically directed at the claim).
2. Therefore claim C is false.

This sort of "reasoning" is fallacious because mocking a claim does not show that it is false. This is especially clear in the following example: "1+1=2! That's the most ridiculous thing I have ever heard!"

It should be noted that showing that a claim is ridiculous through the use of legitimate methods (such as a non-fallacious argument) can make it reasonable to reject the claim. One form of this line of reasoning is known as a "reductio ad absurdum" ("reducing to absurdity"). In this sort of argument, the idea is to show that a contradiction (a statement that must be false) or an absurd result follows from a claim. For example: "Bill claims that a member of a minority group cannot be a racist. However, this is absurd. Think about this: white males are a minority in the world. Given Bill's claim, it would follow that no white males could be racists. Hence, the Klan, Nazis, and white supremacists are not racist organizations."

Since the claim that the Klan, Nazis, and white supremacists are not racist organizations is clearly absurd, it can be concluded that the claim that a member of a minority cannot be a racist is false.

Example#1:
"Sure my worthy opponent claims that we should lower tuition, but that is just laughable."

Example#2:
"Equal rights for women? Yeah, I'll support that when they start paying for dinner and taking out the trash! Hah hah! Fetch me another brewski, Mildred."

Example#3:

"Those crazy conservatives! They think a strong military is the key to peace! Such fools!"

Appeal to Spite

Description:

The Appeal to Spite Fallacy is a fallacy in which spite is substituted for evidence when an "argument" is made against a claim. This line of "reasoning" has the following form:

1. Claim X is presented with the intent of generating spite.
2. Therefore claim C is false (or true)

This sort of "reasoning" is fallacious because a feeling of spite does not count as evidence for or against a claim. This is quite clear in the following case: "Bill claims that the earth revolves around the sun. But remember that dirty trick he pulled on you last week. Now, doesn't my claim that the sun revolves around the earth make sense to you?"

Of course, there are cases in which a claim that evokes a feeling of spite or malice can serve as legitimate evidence. However, it should be noted that the actual feelings of malice or spite are not evidence. The following is an example of such a situation:

Jill: "I think I'll vote for Jane to be treasurer of NOW."
Vicki: "Remember the time that your purse vanished at a meeting last year?"
Jill: "Yes."
Vicki: "Well, I just found out that she stole your purse and stole some other stuff from people."
Jill: "I'm not voting for her!"

In this case, Jill has a good reason not to vote for Jane. Since a treasurer should be honest, a known thief would be a bad choice. As long as Jill concludes that she should vote against Jane because she is a thief and not just out of spite, her reasoning would not be fallacious.

Example #1:

Bill: "I think that Jane did a great job this year. I'm going to nominate her for the award."

Dave: "Have you forgotten last year? Remember that she didn't nominate you last year."
Bill: "You're right. I'm not going to nominate her."

Example #2:
Jill: "I think Jane's idea is a really good one and will really save a lot of money for the department."
Bill: "Maybe. Remember how she showed that your paper had a fatal flaw when you read it at the convention last year…"
Jill: "I had just about forgotten about that! I think I'll go with your idea instead."

Appeal to Tradition

Also Known as: Appeal to the Old, Old Ways are Best, Fallacious Appeal to the Past, Appeal to Age
Description:
　　Appeal to Tradition is a fallacy that occurs when it is assumed that something is better or correct simply because it is older, traditional, or "always has been done." This sort of "reasoning" has the following form:

1. X is old or traditional
2. Therefore X is correct or better.

　　This sort of "reasoning" is fallacious because the age of something does not automatically make it correct or better than something newer. This is made quite obvious by the following example: The theory that witches and demons cause disease is far older than the theory that microorganism cause diseases. Therefore, the theory about witches and demons must be true.
　　This sort of "reasoning" is appealing for a variety of reasons. First, people often prefer to stick with what is older or traditional. This is a fairly common psychological characteristic of people which may stem from the fact that people feel more comfortable about what has been around longer. Second, sticking with things that are older or traditional is often easier than testing new things. Hence, people often prefer older and traditional things out of laziness. Hence, Appeal to Tradition is a somewhat common fallacy.
　　It should not be assumed that new things must be better than old things (see the fallacy Appeal to Novelty) any more than it should be assumed that old things are better than new things. The age of thing does not, in general, have any bearing on its quality or correctness (in this context). In the case of tradition, assuming that

something is correct just because it is considered a tradition is poor reasoning. For example, if the belief that 1+1 = 56 were a tradition of a group of people it would hardly follow that it is true.

Obviously, age does have a bearing in some contexts. For example, if a person concluded that aged wine would be better than brand new wine, he would not be committing an Appeal to Tradition. This is because, in such cases the age of the thing is relevant to its quality. Thus, the fallacy is committed only when the age is not, in and of itself, relevant to the claim.

One final issue that must be considered is the "test of time." In some cases people might be assuming that because something has lasted as a tradition or has been around a long time that it is true because it has "passed the test of time." If a person assumes that something must be correct or true simply because it has persisted a long time, then he has committed an Appeal to Tradition. After all, as history has shown people can persist in accepting false claims for centuries.

However, if a person argues that the claim or thing in question has successfully stood up to challenges and tests for a long period of time then they would not be committing a fallacy. In such cases the claim would be backed by evidence. As an example, the theory that matter is made of subatomic particles has survived numerous tests and challenges over the years so there is a weight of evidence in its favor. The claim is reasonable to accept because of the weight of this evidence and not because the claim is old. Thus, a claim's surviving legitimate challenges and passing valid tests for a long period of time can justify the acceptance of a claim. But mere age or persistence does not warrant accepting a claim.

Example #1:
Sure I believe in God. People have believed in God for thousands of years so it seems clear that God must exist. After all, why else would the belief last so long?

Example #2:
Gunthar is the father of Connan. They live on a small island and in their culture women are treated as property to be exchanged at will by men.

Connan: "You know father, when I was going to school in the United States I saw that American women are not treated as property. In fact, I read a book by this person named Mill in which he argued for women's rights."
Gunthar: "So, what is your point son?"
Connan: "Well, I think that it might be wrong to trade my sisters for cattle. They are human beings and should have a right to be masters of their own fate."
Gunthar: "What a strange and new-fangled notion you picked up in America. That

country must be even more barbaric then I imagined. Now think about this son. We have been trading women for cattle for as long as our people have lived on this island. It is a tradition that goes back into the mists of time. "

Connan: "But I still think there is something wrong with it."

Gunthar: "Nonsense my boy. A tradition this old must be endorsed by the gods and must be right. "

Example #3:

Of course this mode of government is the best. We have had this government for over 200 years and no one has talked about changing it in all that time. So, it has got to be good.

Example #4:

A reporter is interviewing the head of a family that has been involved with a feud with another family.

Reporter: "Mr. Hatfield, why are you still fighting it out with the McCoys?"

Hatfield: "Well you see young man, my father feuded with the McCoys and his father feuded with them and so did my great grandfather."

Reporter: "But why? What started all this?"

Hatfield: "I don't rightly know. I'm sure it was the McCoys who started it all, though."

Reporter: "If you don't know why you're fighting, why don't you just stop?"

Hatfield: "Stop? What are you crazy? This feud has been going on for generations so I'm sure there is a darn good reason why it started. So I aim to keep it going. It has got to be the right thing to do. Hand me my shooting iron boy, I see one of those McCoy skunks sneaking in the cornfield."

Appeal to Silence

Also Known As: Argument from Silence, Argumentum ex Silentio

Description:

   This fallacy occurs when someone attempts to take silence (or a lack of response) as evidence for claim. It has the following form:

1. No reply (or objection) has been made to claim C.

2. Therefore, claim C is true.

This is a fallacy because the fact that no reply (or objection) has been made to a claim is not evidence for that claim. A lack of reply (or objection) leaves the claim with as much evidence as it had prior to any lack of reply (or objection).

There are cases in which a lack of reply (or objection) can be taken as evidence for a claim, but this typically requires establishing a situation in which a lack of reply reasonably indicates consent to accepting the claim. For example, suppose that someone is conducting a meeting in which a matter has been discussed and voted on. The chair says "if there are no objections to be stated, then the consensus is that we will go with Sally's plan." It would not be a fallacy for the chair to accept the claim that the consensus is to go with Sally's plan. While the chair could be mistaken (people might hate her plan but just want the meeting to end), there is no error in reasoning.

This fallacy is similar to appeal to ignorance and is sometimes classified as a variant of this fallacy. The main difference is that an appeal to ignorance is typically based on a general lack of evidence against something while the appeal to silence is typically aimed at the lack of a reply (or objection) in a specific context, such in a conversation or debate in the comments of a blog.

Example #1
"Aha, the blog's author never replied to my criticism of her view of string theory. From her lack of reply, I must infer that she has no reply to make and has conceded to my argument."

Example #2
Eric: "I think that people who are mentally incompetent should not exempt from the death penalty. After all, those are exactly the people we need to get rid of."
Rich: "That is horrible."
Eric: "But can you show I am wrong?"
Rich: "We've been arguing for hours. I'm argued out."
Eric: "Aha! I must be right then."
Rich: "What?"
Eric: "If you have no reply, that means I win. I'm right."
Rich: "Fine."
Eric: "Victory at last!"

Appeal to Vanity

Also Known As: Appeal to Snobbery
Description:
This fallacy occurs when an appeal to vanity or elitism is taken as evidence for a claim. It has the following form:

1. V is presented, with the intent to appeal to the vanity or snobbery of person P.
2. Therefore claim C is true.

This sort of reasoning is fallacious because appealing to a person's vanity or snobbery does not serve as evidence that a claim is true. However, such an appeal can be psychologically effective because people are often swayed by a desire to think of themselves as part of an elite group. This fallacy is most often employed in advertising and the usual tactic is to try to convince people to buy a product because it is associated with someone famous or that having the product somehow makes a person part of a special group.

Example #1
"Ben Affleck wears the finest suits. Of course, he buys then at the Harvard Yard Suit & Baked Bean Emporium. You should too."

Example #2
"Such a fine watch is not for everyone, but only for those who can truly appreciate a majestic time piece. If you are one of the select few, you may arrange an appointment with one of our agents to discuss purchasing opportunities. Needless to say, we do not accept walk-ins."

Argumentum ad Hitlerum

Also Known As: Appeal to Hitler, Reductio ad Hitlerum, the Nazi Argument, the Hitler Card, the Nazi Card, Argument from Hitler
Description:
This fallacy is simply a very specific instance of the general guilt by association fallacy. It has the following general form:

1. Hitler (or some other Nazi, or the Nazis in general) accepts claim C.
2. Therefore claim C is false/wrong.

This is a fallacy for the obvious reason that the mere fact that Hitler (etc.)

accepted a claim (or acted in a certain way) does not show that the claim (or action) is wrong. Hitler certainly believed that 1+1=2 and if this "reasoning" was any good, it would have to be concluded that 1+1 does not equal 2, which is absurd.

While this fallacy is already covered by guilt by association, the excess use of the argumentum ad Hitlerum on the internet, in politics and elsewhere warrants it receiving its own entry.

Example #1

Lee: "So, you are a vegetarian now."

Rachel: "Yes. Well, I am trying."

Lee: "You know that Hitler was a vegetarian, right?"

Rachel: "Really?"

Lee: "Yes. He also hated tobacco smoking."

Rachel: "Quick, get me some bacon and a pack of cigarettes! I repudiate my views!"

Example #2

Ricardo: "Hmm, there seem to be some good arguments for having national health care."

Glenda: "Oh, really?"

Ricardo: "Yes. After all, we have national defense against human enemies and even a federal agency for disasters. Why not have a comparable national defense against diseases and health problems?"

Glenda: "Why not indeed. You know that the Nazis were for national health care. They also killed all those people in the death camps. You are not proposing a final solution to health care, are you?"

Ricardo: "I watch the History Channel, so yeah, I know. But what does that have to do with national health care?"

Glenda: "I'm just connecting the dots."

Ricardo: "Uh huh."

Begging the Question

Also Known as: Circular Reasoning, Reasoning in a Circle, Petitio Principii
Description:

Begging the Question is a fallacy in which the premises include the claim that the conclusion is true or (directly or indirectly) assume that the conclusion is true. This sort of "reasoning" typically has the following form.

1. Premises in which the truth of the conclusion is claimed or the truth of the conclusion is assumed (either directly or indirectly).
2. Claim C (the conclusion) is true.

This sort of "reasoning" is fallacious because simply assuming that the conclusion is true (directly or indirectly) in the premises does not constitute evidence for that conclusion. Obviously, simply assuming a claim is true does not serve as evidence for that claim. This is especially clear in particularly blatant cases: "X is true. The evidence for this claim is that X is true."

Some cases of question begging are fairly blatant, while others can be extremely subtle.

Example #1:
Bill: "God must exist."
Jill: "How do you know."
Bill: "Because the Bible says so."
Jill: "Why should I believe the Bible?"
Bill: "Because the Bible was written by God."

Example #2:
"If such actions were not illegal , then they would not be prohibited by the law."

Example #3:
"The belief in God is universal. After all, everyone believes in God."

Example #4:
Interviewer: "Your resume looks impressive but I need another reference."
Bill: "Jill can give me a good reference."
Interviewer: "Good. But how do I know that Jill is trustworthy?"
Bill: "Certainly. I can vouch for her."

Biased Generalization

Also Known as: Biased Statistics, Loaded Sample, Prejudiced Statistics, Prejudiced Sample, Loaded Statistics, Biased Induction, Biased Generalization
Description:
This fallacy is committed when a person draws a conclusion about a population

based on a sample that is biased or prejudiced in some manner. It has the following form:

1. Sample S, which is biased, is taken from population P.
2. Conclusion C is drawn about Population P based on S.

The person committing the fallacy is misusing the following type of reasoning, which is known variously as Inductive Generalization, Generalization, and Statistical Generalization:

1. X% of all observed A's are B's.
2. Therefore X% of all A's are B's.

The fallacy is committed when the sample of A's is likely to be biased in some manner. A sample is biased or loaded when the method used to take the sample is likely to result in a sample that does not adequately represent the population from which it is drawn.

Biased samples are generally not very reliable. As a blatant case, imagine that a person is taking a sample from a truckload of small colored balls, some of which are metal and some of which are plastic. If he used a magnet to select his sample, then his sample would include a disproportionate number of metal balls (after all, the sample will probably be made up entirely of the metal balls). In this case, any conclusions he might draw about the whole population of balls would be unreliable since he would have few or no plastic balls in the sample.

The general idea is that biased samples are less likely to contain numbers proportional to the whole population. For example, if a person wants to find out what most Americans thought about gun control, a poll taken at an NRA meeting would be a biased sample.

Since the Biased Sample fallacy is committed when the sample (the observed instances) is biased or loaded, it is important to have samples that are not biased making a generalization. The best way to do this is to take samples in ways that avoid bias. There are, in general, three types of samples that are aimed at avoiding bias. The general idea is that these methods (when used properly) will result in a sample that matches the whole population fairly closely. The three types of samples are as follows

Random Sample: This is a sample that is taken in such a way that nothing but chance determines which members of the population are selected for the sample. Ideally, any individual member of the population has the same chance as being selected as any other. This type of sample avoids being biased because a biased sample is one that is taken in such a way that some members of the population have a significantly greater chance of being selected for the sample than other members. Unfortunately, creating an ideal random sample is often very difficult.

Stratified Sample: This is a sample that is taken by using the following steps: 1) The relevant strata (population subgroups) are identified, 2) The number of members in each stratum is determined and 3) A random sample is taken from each stratum in exact proportion to its size. This method is obviously most useful when dealing with stratified populations. For example, a person's income often influences how she votes, so when conducting a presidential poll it would be a good idea to take a stratified sample using economic classes as the basis for determining the strata. This method avoids loaded samples by (ideally) ensuring that each stratum of the population is adequately represented.

Time Lapse Sample: This type of sample is taken by taking a stratified or random sample and then taking at least one more sample with a significant lapse of time between them. After the two samples are taken, they can be compared for changes. This method of sample taking is very important when making predictions. A prediction based on only one sample is likely to be a Hasty Generalization (because the sample is likely to be too small to cover past, present and future populations) or a Biased Sample (because the sample will only include instances from one time period)

People often commit Biased Sample because of bias or prejudice. For example, a person might intentionally or unintentionally seek out people or events that support his bias. As an example, a person who is pushing a particular scientific theory might tend to gather samples that are biased in favor of that theory.

People also commonly commit this fallacy because of laziness or sloppiness. It is very easy to simply take a sample from what happens to be easily available rather than taking the time and effort to generate an adequate sample and draw a justified conclusion.

It is important to keep in mind that bias is relative to the purpose of the sample. For example, if Bill wanted to know what NRA members thought about a gun control law, then taking a sample at a NRA meeting would not be biased. However, if Bill wanted to determine what Americans in general thought about the law, then a sample taken at an NRA meeting would be biased.

Example #1:
Bill is assigned by his editor to determine what most Americans think about a new law that will place a federal tax on all modems and computers purchased. The revenues from the tax will be used to enforce new online decency laws. Bill, being

technically inclined, decides to use an email poll. In his poll, 95% of those surveyed opposed the tax. Bill was quite surprised when 65% of all Americans voted for the taxes.

Example #2:
The United Pacifists of America decide to run a poll to determine what Americans think about guns and gun control. Jane is assigned the task of setting up the study. To save mailing costs, she includes the survey form in the group's newsletter mailing. She is very pleased to find out that 95% of those surveyed favor gun control laws and she tells her friends that the vast majority of Americans favor gun control laws.

Example #3:
Large scale polls were taken in Florida, California, and Maine and it was found that an average of 55% of those polled spent at least fourteen days a year near the ocean. So, it can be safely concluded that 55% of all Americans spend at least fourteen days near the ocean each year.

Burden of Proof

Also Known As: Appeal to Ignorance, Ad Ignorantiam
Description:
   Burden of Proof is a fallacy in which the burden of proof is placed on the wrong side. Another version occurs when a lack of evidence for side A is taken to be evidence for side B in cases in which the burden of proof actually rests on side B. A common name for this is an Appeal to Ignorance. This sort of reasoning typically has the following form:

1. Claim X is presented by side A and the burden of proof actually rests on side B.
2. Side B claims that X is false because there is no proof for X.

   In many situations, one side has the burden of proof resting on it. This side is obligated to provide evidence for its position. The claim of the other side, the one that does not bear the burden of proof, is assumed to be true unless proven otherwise. The difficulty in such cases is determining which side, if any, the burden of proof rests on. In many cases, settling this issue can be a matter of significant debate. In some cases the burden of proof is set by the situation. For example, in American law a person is assumed to be innocent until proven guilty (hence the burden of proof is on the prosecution). As another example, in debate the burden of proof is placed on the affirmative team. As a final example, in most cases the burden of proof rests on those who claim something exists (such as Bigfoot, psychic powers, universals, and sense data).

Example #1:
Bill: "I think that we should invest more money in expanding the interstate system."
Jill: "I think that would be a bad idea, considering the state of the treasury."
Bill: How can anyone be against highway improvements?"

Example #2:
Bill: "I think that some people have psychic powers."
Jill: "What is your proof?"
Bill: "No one has been able to prove that people do not have psychic powers."

Example #3:
"You cannot prove that God does not exist, so He does."

Complex Question

Description:
This fallacy is committed by attempting to support a claim by presenting a question that rests on one or more unwarranted assumptions. The fallacy has the following form:

1. Question Q is asked which rests on assumption (or assumptions) A.
2. Therefore A is true.

This version of the fallacy is similar to begging the question in that what is in need of proof is assumed rather than properly established.

Complex question is also often defined as presenting two or more questions as if they were a single question and then using the answer to the single question to answer both questions. The answer is then used as a premise to support a conclusion. This version has the following form:

1. Question Q is presented that is actually formed of two (or more) questions Q1 and Q2 (etc.).
2. Question Q is based on one or more unwarranted assumptions, U.
3. An answer, A, is received to Q and treated as if it answers Q1 and Q2.

4. On the basis of A, U is concluded to be true.

This is a fallacy because the answer, A, is acquired on the basis of one or more unwarranted assumptions. As such, the conclusion is not adequately supported.

This fallacy needs to be distinguished from the rhetorical technique of the loaded question. In this technique a question is raised that rests on one or more unwarranted assumptions, but there is no attempt to make an argument. In the context of law, a loaded question is sometimes referred to as a leading question. The classic example of a loaded question is "have you stopped beating your wife?"

Example #1
"How can America be saved from the socialist programs and job killing ways of the current administration? Clearly there is only one way: vote Republican!"

Example #2
Professor: "Have you stopped plagiarizing papers?"
George: "Um, Yes."
Professor: "Ah, that means that you were plagiarizing papers and that you have stopped now!"
George: "What?!"
Professor: "Well, you said you had stopped. That requires that you had been plagiarizing before. You could not very well stop if you had not started, right?"
George: "Um, I mean that no, I haven't stopped."
Professor: "Aha, so you are still plagiarizing papers! If you have not stopped, that means you have been and still are plagiarizing away!"
George: "No, I mean…I don't know what I mean!"
Sally: "George, you got suckered into that. The right answer is to say 'no, I didn't stop because I never started.'"

Example #3
Lawyer: "So where did you hide the money that was stolen in the robbery?"
Defendant: "Nowhere."
Lawyer: "Ah, so you did not hide it. It must then be inferred that you spent it all."
Defendant: "What, I didn't steal the money!"
Lawyer: "But you just said that you hid it nowhere. That seems to be an admission of guilt!"
Defendant: "Hey, shouldn't my lawyer be objecting or something?"
Lawyer: "Even he can see you are guilty."

Composition, Fallacy of

Description:

The fallacy of Composition is committed when a conclusion is drawn about a whole based on the features of its constituents when, in fact, no justification provided for the inference. There are actually two types of this fallacy, both of which are known by the same name (because of the high degree of similarity).

The first type of fallacy of Composition arises when a person reasons from the characteristics of individual members of a class or group to a conclusion regarding the characteristics of the entire class or group (taken as a whole). More formally, the "reasoning" would look something like this.

1. Individual F things have characteristics A, B, C, etc.
2. Therefore, the (whole) class of F things has characteristics A, B, C, etc.

This line of reasoning is fallacious because the mere fact that individuals have certain characteristics does not, in itself, guarantee that the class (taken as a whole) has those characteristics.

It is important to note that drawing an inference about the characteristics of a class based on the characteristics of its individual members is not always fallacious. In some cases, sufficient justification can be provided to warrant the conclusion. For example, it is true that an individual rich person has more wealth than an individual poor person. In some nations (such as the US) it is true that the class of wealthy people has more wealth as a whole than does the class of poor people. In this case, the evidence used would warrant the inference and the fallacy of Composition would not be committed.

The second type of fallacy of Composition is committed when it is concluded that what is true of the parts of a whole must be true of the whole without there being adequate justification for the claim. More formally, the line of "reasoning" would be as follows:

1. The parts of the whole X have characteristics A, B, C, etc.
2. Therefore the whole X must have characteristics A, B, C.

This sort of reasoning is fallacious because it cannot be inferred that simply because the parts of a complex whole have (or lack) certain properties that the whole that they are parts of has those properties. This is especially clear in math:

The numbers 1 and 3 are both odd. 1 and 3 are parts of 4. Therefore, the number 4 is odd.

It must be noted that reasoning from the properties of the parts to the properties of the whole is not always fallacious. If there is justification for the inference from parts to whole, then the reasoning is not fallacious. For example, if every part of the human body is made of matter, then it would not be an error in reasoning to conclude that the whole human body is made of matter. Similarly, if every part of a structure is made of brick, there is no fallacy committed when one concludes that the whole structure is made of brick.

Example #1:
A main battle tank uses more fuel than a car. Therefore, the main battle tanks use up more of the available fuel in the world than do all the cars.

Example #2:
A tiger eats more food than a human being. Therefore, tigers, as a group, eat more food than do all the humans on the earth.

Example #3:
Atoms are colorless. Cats are made of atoms, so cats are colorless.

Example #4:
Every player on the team is a superstar and a great player, so the team is a great team." This is fallacious since the superstars might not be able to play together very well and hence they could be a lousy team.

Example #5:
Each part of the show, from the special effects to the acting is a masterpiece. So, the whole show is a masterpiece." This is fallacious since a show could have great acting, great special effects and such, yet still fail to "come together" to make a masterpiece.

Example #6:
Come on, you like beef, potatoes, and green beans, so you will like this beef, potato, and green bean casserole." This is fallacious for the same reason that the following is fallacious: "You like eggs, ice cream, pizza, cake, fish, jello, chicken, taco sauce, soda, oranges, milk, egg rolls, and yogurt so you must like this yummy dish made out of all of them.

Example #7:
Sodium and chlorine are both dangerous to humans. Therefore any combination of sodium and chlorine will be dangerous to humans.

Confusing Cause and Effect

Also Known as: Questionable Cause, Reversing Causation
Description:
 Confusing Cause and Effect is a fallacy that has the following general form:

1. A and B regularly occur together.
2. Therefore A is the cause of B.

 This fallacy requires that there not be, in fact, a common cause that actually causes both A and B.
 This fallacy is committed when a person assumes that one event must cause another just because the events occur together. More formally, this fallacy involves drawing the conclusion that A is the cause of B simply because A and B are in regular conjunction (and there is not a common cause that is actually the cause of A and B). The mistake being made is that the causal conclusion is being drawn without adequate justification.
 In some cases it will be evident that the fallacy is being committed. For example, a person might claim that an illness was caused by a person getting a fever. In this case, it would be quite clear that the fever was caused by illness and not the other way around. In other cases, the fallacy is not always evident. One factor that makes causal reasoning quite difficult is that it is not always evident what is the cause and what is the effect. For example, a problem child might be the cause of the parents being short tempered or the short temper of the parents might be the cause of the child being problematic. The difficulty is increased by the fact that some situations might involve feedback. For example, the parents' temper might cause the child to become problematic and the child's behavior could worsen the parents' temper. In such cases it could be rather difficult to sort out what caused what in the first place.
 In order to determine that the fallacy has been committed, it must be shown that the causal conclusion has not been adequately supported and that the person committing the fallacy has confused the actual cause with the effect. Showing that the fallacy has been committed will typically involve determining the actual cause and the actual effect. In some cases, as noted above, this can be quite easy. In other cases it will be difficult. In some cases, it might be almost impossible. Another thing that makes causal reasoning difficult is that people often have very different

conceptions of cause and, in some cases, the issues are clouded by emotions and ideologies. For example, people often claim violence on TV and in movies must be censored because it causes people to like violence. Other people claim that there is violence on TV and in movies because people like violence. In this case, it is not obvious what the cause really is and the issue is clouded by the fact that emotions often run high on this issue.

While causal reasoning can be difficult, many errors can be avoided with due care and careful testing procedures. This is due to the fact that the fallacy arises because the conclusion is drawn without due care. One way to avoid the fallacy is to pay careful attention to the temporal sequence of events. Since (outside of Star Trek), effects do not generally precede their causes, if A occurs after B, then A cannot be the cause of B. However, these methods go beyond the scope of this program.

All causal fallacies involve an error in causal reasoning. However, this fallacy differs from the other causal fallacies in terms of the error in reasoning being made. In the case of a Post Hoc fallacy, the error is that a person is accepting that A is the cause of B simply because A occurs before B. In the case of the Fallacy of Ignoring a Common Cause A is taken to be the cause of B when there is, in fact, a third factor that is the cause of both A and B. For more information, see the relevant entries in this program.

Example #1:

Bill and Joe are having a debate about music and moral decay:

Bill: '"It seems clear to me that this new music is causing the youth to become corrupt."

Joe: 'What do you mean?"

Bill: "This rap stuff is always telling the kids to kill cops, do drugs, and abuse women. That is all bad and the kids today shouldn't be doing that sort of stuff. We ought to ban that music!"

Joe: "So, you think that getting rid of the rap music would solve the drug, violence and sexism problems in the US?"

Bill: "Well, it wouldn't get rid of it all, but it would take care of a lot of it."

Joe: "Don't you think that most of the rap singers sing about that sort of stuff because that is what is really going on these days? I mean, people often sing about the conditions of their time, just like the people did in the sixties. But then I suppose that you think that people were against the war and into drugs just because they listened to Dylan and Baez."

Bill: "Well…"

Joe: "Well, it seems to me that the main cause of the content of the rap music is the pre-existing social conditions. If there weren't all these problems, the rap singers probably wouldn't be singing about them. I also think that if the social conditions were great, kids could listen to the music all day and not be affected."

Joe: 'Well, I still think the rap music causes the problems. You can't argue against the fact that social ills really picked up at the same time rap music got started."

Example #2:
It is claimed by some people that severe illness is caused by depression and anger. After all, people who are severely ill are very often depressed and angry. Thus, it follows that the cause of severe illness actually is the depression and anger. So, a good and cheerful attitude is key to staying healthy.

Example #3:
Bill sets out several plates with bread on them. After a couple days, he notices that the bread has mold growing all over it. Bill concludes that the mold was produced by the bread going bad. When Bill tells his mother about his experiment, she tells him that the mold was the cause of the bread going bad and that he better clean up the mess if he wants to get his allowance this week.

Confusing Explanations and Excuses

Description:
   This fallacy occurs when it is uncritically assumed that an explanation given for an action is an attempt to excuse or justify it. This fallacy has the following form:

1. Explanation E is offered for action A.
2. Therefore E is an attempt to excuse or justify A.

   This is a fallacy because an explanation of an action need not involve any attempt to excuse or justify that action.
   This fallacy can be committed by accident due to a failure to distinguish between an explanation and an excuse or justification. This most often occurs because people confuse explanations and arguments. Explanations are attempts to provide an account as to how or why something is the case or how it works. Arguments, in the logical sense, are attempts to establish that a claim (the conclusion) is true by providing reasons or evidence (premises). What can add to the confusion is the fact that explanations can be used in arguments, generally to establish an excuse or to justify an action.
   To illustrate, if someone said, "John missed class because he was in a car wreck", this would be an explanation rather than an argument. However, if someone said,

"John's absence from class should be excused because he was in a car wreck", then this would be an argument. This is because John being in a car wreck is being offered as a reason why his absence should be excused.

The fallacy can also be committed intentionally in an attempt to "prove" that someone is trying to justify an action when they are actually only offering an explanation.

It is also a mistake to assume that an excuse or justification is only an explanation, although that sort of error is not nearly as common as confusing explanations with excuses.

Example #1

Hosni: "While it has been common for many American politicians to claim that terrorists attacked America because they hate our freedoms, the reality seems to be that they have been primarily motivated by American foreign policy."
Sam: "I can't believe that you are defending the terrorists! How can you say that the 9/11 attack was justified?"
Hosni: "I said no such thing."
Sam: "Yeah, you did. You said that they were motivated by American foreign policy. That means you think we made them attack us and they were right to do so!"

Example #2

Karen: "I think that Bill is doing badly in the class because he finds the subject matter boring. During my recitation sections he just spends his time texting, no matter how often I ask him not to. I know he can do good work-my sister showed me some of his work in his major, and it is really good. But my sister says that he's not interested in philosophy."
Drew: "I know that Bill is your sister's boyfriend, but you don't have to defend him."
Karen: "I'm not. I'm just saying why he is doing badly."
Drew: "Don't get defensive. I'm fine with teaching assistants who advocate for students. I was quite the advocate in my day, you know."
Karen: "Really?"
Drew: "Of course. Now I'm the cruel professor. Hah, hah."
Karen: "Hah."

Circumstantial Ad Hominem

Description:

A Circumstantial ad Hominem is a fallacy in which one attempts to attack a claim by asserting that the person making the claim is making it simply out of self-interest. In some cases, this fallacy involves substituting an attack on a person's circumstances (such as the person's religion, political affiliation, ethnic background, etc.). The fallacy has the following forms:

Form 1
1. Person A makes claim X.
2. Person B asserts that A makes claim X because it is in A's interest to claim X.
3. Therefore claim X is false.

Form 2
1. Person A makes claim X.
2. Person B makes an attack on A's circumstances.
3. Therefore X is false.

A Circumstantial ad Hominem is a fallacy because a person's interests and circumstances have no bearing on the truth or falsity of the claim being made. While a person's interests will provide them with motives to support certain claims, the claims stand or fall on their own. It is also the case that a person's circumstances (religion, political affiliation, etc.) do not affect the truth or falsity of the claim. This is made quite clear by the following example: "Bill claims that 1+1 =2. But he is a Republican, so his claim is false."

There are times when it is prudent to suspicious of a person's claims, such as when it is evident that the claims are being biased by the person's interests. For example, if a tobacco company representative claims that tobacco does not cause cancer, it would be prudent to not simply accept the claim. This is because the person has a motivation to make the claim, whether it is true or not. However, the mere fact that the person has a motivation to make the claim does not make it false. For example, suppose a parent tells her son that sticking a fork in a light socket would be dangerous. Simply because she has a motivation to say this obviously does not make her claim false.

Example #1:
"She asserts that we need more military spending, but that is false, since she is only saying it because she is a Republican."

Example #2:
"I think that we should reject what Father Jones has to say about the ethical issues of abortion because he is a Catholic priest. After all, Father Jones is required to hold such views."

Example #3:
"Of course the Senator from Maine opposes a reduction in naval spending. After all, Bath Ironworks, which produces warships, is in Maine."

Example #4:
"Bill claims that tax breaks for corporations increases development. Of course, Bill is the CEO of a corporation."

Cum Hoc, Ergo Propter Hoc

Description:

This is an error in causal reasoning that occurs when it is assumed that the correlation between two things must be a causal connection. Translated into English, it means "with that, therefore because of that." This fallacy has the following form:

1. There is a correlation between A and B.
2. Therefore, A causes B.

This fallacy is related to the post hoc ergo propter hoc fallacy. The difference is that the post hoc fallacy occurs when it is inferred that A causes B merely because A occurs before B. In the cum hoc fallacy, the error involves assuming that correlation must entail causation.

Obviously enough, the fact that two things are correlated is not enough to justify inferring that there is a causal connection. In some cases, this is rather obvious. For example, (almost) no one would infer that winter is caused by people wearing winter jackets.

Not surprisingly, the fallacy occurs most often when it seems like there might be a connection between the things. For example, a person might find that there is a correlation between sleeping fully dressed and waking up with a headache and conclude that sleeping clothed causes headaches. The fallacy can even be committed when there really is a causal connection between the two things. While this might seem odd, the key to the fallacy is not that there is no causal connection between A and B. It is that adequate evidence has not been provided for the claim that A causes B.

This fallacy is typically committed because people are simply not careful enough when they reason. Leaping to a causal conclusion is always easier and faster than actually investigating the phenomenon. However, such leaps tend to land far from the truth of the matter. Because this fallacy is committed by drawing an unjustified causal conclusion, the key to avoiding them is careful investigation. While it is true that causes and effects are in correlation, it is not true that correlation makes something a cause of something else. Because of this, a causal investigation can start by an investigation of correlation, but it should not end there.

Example#1

"You know what I've noticed? There is a correlation between when the President speaks on the economy and the Dow Jones. While it does not happen every single time, usually when he speaks the Jones dips. And the more he talks, the deeper the dip. If he wants to help the economy, he needs to stop talking about it-his speeches are bringing it down!"

Example #2

Sam: "After four years of college I've learned something important."
Jane: "And what might that be, Socrates?"
Sam: "Sleeping in your clothes gives me a headache."
Jane: "You've been sleeping in my clothes?"
Sam: "No, I mean the general thing. Well, I mean when I sleep in my clothes I get a headache. I'm not sure why, but sleeping with clothes on hurts my head. So that is why I started sleeping naked."
Jane: "What does your roommate think of that?"
Sam: "He's not happy. He calls me 'junk man.'"
Jane: "So, do you no longer get headaches?"
Sam: "That is the odd part. I still do. But I'm sure the clothes cause headaches. Maybe I'm sleeping too close to them?"
Jane: "Yeah, I'm sure that is it."

Example #3

Ashleigh: "I've decided I'm not eating ice cream before I go swimming."
Nancy: "You know that isn't true. The myth about eating before swimming, I mean."
Ashleigh: "Oh, I know. But I heard the professor say in class that drowning deaths increase in proportion to the sale of ice cream. I'm not sure what he was talking about, but I'm fairly sure that eating ice cream before swimming would be risky."

Division, Fallacy of

Description:

The fallacy of Division is committed when a person infers that what is true of a whole must also be true of its constituents and justification for that inference is not provided. There are two main variants of the general fallacy of Division:

The first type of fallacy of Division is committed when 1) a person reasons that what is true of the whole must also be true of the parts and 2) the person fails to justify that inference with the required degree of evidence. More formally, the "reasoning" follows this sort of pattern:

1. The whole, X, has properties A, B, C, etc.
2. Therefore the parts of X have properties A,B,C, etc.

That this line of reasoning is fallacious is made clear by the following case: 4 is an even number. 1 and 3 are parts of 4. Therefore 1 and 3 are even.

It should be noted that it is not always fallacious to draw a conclusion about the parts of a whole based on the properties of the whole. As long as adequate evidence is provided in the argument, the reasoning can be acceptable. For example, the human body is made out of matter and it is reasonable to infer from this that the parts that make up the human body are also made out of matter. This is because there is no reason to believe that the body is made up of non-material parts that somehow form matter when they get together.

The second version of the fallacy of division is committed when a person 1) draws a conclusion about the properties of individual members of a class or group based on the collective properties of the class or group and 2) there is not enough justification for the conclusion. More formally, the line of "reasoning" is as follows:

1. As a collective, group or class X has properties A,B,C, etc.
2. Therefore the individual members of group or class X have properties A,B,C, etc.

That this sort of reasoning is fallacious can be easily shown by the following: It is true that athletes, taken as a group, are football players, track runners, swimmers, tennis players, long jumpers, pole vaulters and such. But it would be fallacious to infer that each individual athlete is a football player, a track runner, a swimmer, a tennis player, a swimmer, etc.

It should be noted that it is not always fallacious to draw a conclusion about an individual based on what is true of the class he/she/it belongs to. If the inference is backed by evidence, then the reasoning can be fine. For example, it is not fallacious to infer that Bill the Siamese cat is a mammal from the fact that all cats are mammals. In this case, what is true of the class is also true of each individual member.

Example #1:
"The ball is blue, therefore the atoms that make it up are also blue."

Example #2:
"A living cell is organic material, so the chemicals making up the cell must also be organic material."

Example #3:
"Bill lives in a large building, so his apartment must be large."

Example #4:
"Sodium chloride (table salt) may be safely eaten. Therefore its constituent elements, sodium and chlorine, may be safely eaten."

Example #5:
"Americans use much more electricity than Africans do. So Bill, who lives in primitive cabin in Maine, uses more electricity than Nelson, who lives in a modern house in South Africa. "

Example #6:
"Men receive more higher education than women. Therefore Dr. Jane Smart has less higher education than Mr. Bill Buffoon. "

Example #7:
"Minorities get paid less than whites in America. Therefore, the black CEO of a multi-billion dollar company gets paid less than the white janitor who cleans his office."

Equivocation, Fallacy of

Description:

Equivocation occurs when an ambiguous expression is used in more than one of its meanings in a single context. The fallacy occurs when that context is an argument and the conclusion depends on shifting the meaning of the expression while treating it as if it remains the same.

1. A premise or premises are presented that contain an equivocation.
2. Conclusion C is drawn from these premises.

Ambiguity by itself is not fallacious, but is a lack of clarity in language that occurs when a claim has two (or more) meanings and it is not clear which is intended. The sort of "reasoning" presented above is fallacious because the evidence merely appears to support the conclusion since the same word is being used. Because the word shifts in meaning, the evidence does not actually support the conclusion.

In some cases the error is obvious. For example, if someone said "Sally is standing on my right, I'm a moderate and people to the right of me are conservative, so Sally is a conservative", then most people would not fall for this line of "reasoning" and would probably regard it as a lame joke. Other cases of equivocation, especially ones that occur with a more subtle equivocation, can be far more tempting.

Equivocation, like amphiboly, is often used in humor. Such uses are not intended as serious arguments and would not (generally) count as fallacies. Perhaps the most famous example is from Alice in Wonderland:

Who did you pass on the road?' the King went on, holding out his hand to the Messenger for some more hay.

'Nobody,' said the Messenger.

'Quite right,' said the King: 'this young lady saw him too. So of course Nobody walks slower than you.

'I do my best,' the Messenger said in a sulky tone. 'I'm sure nobody walks much faster than I do!'

'He can't do that,' said the King, 'or else he'd have been here first. However, now you've got your breath, you may tell us what's happened in the town.'

Example #1

"A blue whale is an animal, therefore a small blue whale is a small animal."

Example #2

"A feather is light. What is light is not dark. So, feathers cannot be dark."

Example #3

Rex: "I can't believe that Sally still doesn't believe me."
Ted: "Why not?"
Rex: "Well, I gave her the reason why I did it and I learned in logic that reasons support claims. So, she should believe me."

Example #4

"Every day we see miracles such as antibiotics, the internet, and space travel. So when those atheists say there are no miracles, they are wrong. So, that pretty much wraps it up for the atheists' claim."

Fallacious Example

Also Known As: Fallacious Argument by/from Example
Description:

This fallacy occurs when an argument by/from example fails to adequately meet the standards for assessing said argument type.

Not surprisingly, an argument by example is an argument in which a claim is supported by providing examples.

Strictly presented, an argument by/from example will have at least one premise and a conclusion. Each premise is used to support the conclusion by providing an example. The general idea is that the weight of the examples establishes the claim in question.

Although people generally present arguments by example in a fairly informal manner, they have the following logical form:

1. Premise 1: Example 1 is an example that supports claim P.
2. Premise n: Example n is an example that supports claim P.
3. Conclusion: Claim P is true.

In this case *n* is a variable standing for the number of the premise in question and P is a variable standing for the claim under consideration.

An example of an argument by example presented in strict form is as follows:

Premise 1: Lena ate pizza two months ago and did not contribute any money.
Premise 2: Lena ate pizza a month ago and did not contribute any money.

Premise 3: Lena ate pizza two weeks ago and did not contribute any money.
Premise 4: Lena ate pizza a week ago and did not contribute any money.
Conclusion: Lena is a pizza mooch who eats but does not contribute.

Standards of Assessment

The strength of an argument by/from example depends on four factors First, the more examples, the stronger the argument. For example, if Lena only failed to pay for the pizza she ate once, then the claim that she is a mooch who does not contribute would not be well supported-the argument would be very weak.

Second, the more relevant the examples, the stronger the argument. For example, if it were concluded that Lena was a pizza mooch because she regularly failed to pay for her share of gas money, then the argument would be fairly weak. After all, her failure to pay gas money does not strongly support the claim that she won't help pay for pizza (although it would provide grounds for suspecting she might not pay).

Third, the examples must be specific and clearly identified. Vague and unidentified examples do not provide much in the way of support. For example, if someone claimed that Lena was a pizza mooch because "you know, she didn't pay and stuff on some days…like some time a month or maybe a couple months ago", then the argument would be extremely weak.

Fourth, counter-examples must be considered. A counter-example is an example that counts against the claim. One way to look at a counter example is that it is an example that supports the denial of the conclusion being argued for. The more counter-examples and the more relevant they are, the weaker the argument. For example, if someone accuses Lena of being a pizza mooch, but other people have examples of times which she did contribute, then these examples would serve as counter-examples against the claim that she is a pizza mooch. As such, counter-examples can be used to build an argument by example that has as its conclusion the claim that the conclusion it counters is false.

An argument that does not meet these standards would be a weak argument. If the argument is weak enough (though there is not an exact line that defines this) it would qualify as a fallacy because the premises would not adequately support the conclusion.

Example #1

Rush: "The President is a socialist!"
Sean: "Really? Can you prove that?"
Rush: "Well he did those things, you know like that money thing and that other thing with insurance. You know, the socialist things."

Sean: "So, those examples prove he is a socialist?"
Rush: "Well, yeah."

Example #2
Dan: "In the Apology, Socrates argues that he did not corrupt the youth intentionally. He does this by asserting that if he corrupted them, they would probably hurt him. But, since no one wants to be harmed, he would not corrupt them intentionally. However, there are plenty of examples of leaders who corrupted their followers without being harmed by them. So much for Socrates' argument!"
Ted: "Like who?"
Dan: "You know, like those leaders that corrupted people."
Ted: "Oh, them."

Fallacy Fallacy

Also Known As: Argumentum ad Logicam, Fallacist's Fallacy
Description:
   This fallacy occurs when someone infers that a claim is false because a fallacy has been used to "support" that claim. The form of this "reasoning" is as follows:

1. Fallacy F was used to argue for claim C.
2. Therefore claim C is false.

   This is a fallacy (and a somewhat ironic one) because the truth or falsity of a claim cannot be inferred solely from the quality of the reasoning. If someone has committed a fallacy, then he has made an error in reasoning but it does not follow that he has made a factual error. As noted above, it is one thing to commit an error in reasoning and quite another to get the facts wrong. One does not follow from the other.
   This is especially clear when a deductive fallacy (an invalid deductive argument) is considered:

1. If Washington D.C. is the capital of the United States, then it is in the United States.
2. Washington D.C. is in the United States.
3. Conclusion: Washington D.C. is the capital of the United States.

This is an example of the famous deductive fallacy affirming the consequent and is invalid. However, the conclusion is true. As such, it should be clear that poor reasoning does not entail a false conclusion.

Example #1

Glenn: "Obama is a Muslim and a socialist. That is why he is wrong when he claims his stimulus plan helped the economy."

Jon: "Aha! I just read about fallacies on the internet and you, my fine fellow, have just committed an ad hominem! That means that you are wrong: Obama's plan must have helped the economy."

Example #2

Sally: "Why should you believe in God? Well, the bible says that God exists."

Jane: "But why should I believe the bible? It is just a book after all."

Sally: "It was written by God, so you can believe every word."

Jane: "Hey, you are just assuming what you need to prove. That isn't a good argument at all! So, that just about wraps it up for God."

Jane: "What?"

Sally: "Well, your argument is bad, so your conclusion has to be wrong."

Jane: "I don't think it works that way."

Sally: "Why, did God put that in His book?"

False Dilemma

Also Known as: Black & White Thinking
Description:

A False Dilemma is a fallacy in which a person uses the following pattern of "reasoning":

1. Either claim X is true or claim Y is true (when X and Y could both be false).
2. Claim Y is false.
3. Therefore claim X is true.

This line of "reasoning" is fallacious because if both claims could be false, then it cannot be inferred that one is true because the other is false. That this is the case is made clear by the following example:

1. Either 1+1 =4 or 1+1=12 .
2. It is not the case that 1+1 = 4.
3. Therefore 1+1 =12.

In cases in which the two options are, in fact, the only two options, this line of reasoning is not fallacious. For example:

1. Bill is dead or he is alive.
2. Bill is not dead.
3. Therefore Bill is alive.

Example #1:
Senator Jill: "We'll have to cut education funding this year."
Senator Bill" "Why?"
Senator Jill: "Well, either we cut the social programs or we live with a huge deficit and we can't live with the deficit."

Example #2:
Bill: "Jill and I both support having prayer in public schools."
Jill: "Hey, I never said that!"
Bill: "You're not an atheist are you Jill?

Example #3:
"Look, you are going to have to make up your mind. Either you decide that you can afford this stereo, or you decide you are going to do without music for a while."

Gambler's Fallacy

Description:
The Gambler's Fallacy is committed when a person assumes that a departure from what occurs on average or in the long term will be corrected in the short term. The form of the fallacy is as follows:

1. X has happened.
2. X departs from what is expected to occur on average or over the long term.
3. Therefore, X will come to an end soon.

There are two common ways this fallacy is committed. In both cases a person is assuming that some result must be "due" simply because what has previously happened departs from what would be expected on average or over the long term.

The first involves events whose probabilities of occurring are independent of one another. For example, one toss of a fair (two sides, non-loaded) coin does not affect the next toss of the coin. So, each time the coin is tossed there is (ideally) a 50% chance of it landing heads and a 50% chance of it landing tails. Suppose that a person tosses a coin 6 times and gets a head each time. If he concludes that the next toss will be tails because tails "is due", then he will have committed the Gambler's Fallacy. This is because the results of previous tosses have no bearing on the outcome of the 7th toss. It has a 50% chance of being heads and a 50% chance of being tails, just like any other toss.

The second involves cases whose probabilities of occurring are not independent of one another. For example, suppose that a boxer has won 50% of his fights over the past two years. Suppose that after several fights he has won 50% of his matches this year, that he has lost his last six fights and he has six left. If a person believed that he would win his next six fights because he has used up his losses and is "due" for a victory, then he would have committed the Gambler's Fallacy. After all, the person would be ignoring the fact that the results of one match can influence the results of the next one. For example, the boxer might have been injured in one match which would lower his chances of winning his last six fights.

It should be noted that not all predictions about what is likely to occur are fallacious. If a person has good evidence for his predictions, then they will be reasonable to accept. For example, if a person tosses a fair coin and gets nine heads in a row it would be reasonable for him to conclude that he will probably not get another nine in a row again. This reasoning would not be fallacious as long as he believed his conclusion because of an understanding of the laws of probability. In this case, if he concluded that he would not get another nine heads in a row because the odds of getting nine heads in a row are lower than getting fewer than nine heads in a row, then his reasoning would be good and his conclusion would be justified. Hence, determining whether or not the Gambler's Fallacy is being committed often requires some basic understanding of the laws of probability.

Example #1:
Bill is playing against Doug in a WWII tank battle game. Doug has had a great "streak of luck" and has been killing Bill's tanks left and right with good die rolls. Bill, who has a few tanks left, decides to risk all in a desperate attack on Doug. He is a bit worried that Doug might wipe him out, but he thinks that since Doug's luck at rolling has been great Doug must be due for some bad dice rolls. Bill launches his attack and Doug butchers his forces.

Example #2:
Jane and Bill are talking:

Jane: "I'll be able to buy that car I always wanted soon."
Bill: "Why, did you get a raise?"
Jane: "No. But you know how I've been playing the lottery all these years?"
Bill: "Yes, you buy a ticket for every drawing, without fail."
Jane: "And I've lost every time."
Bill: "So why do you think you will win this time?"
Jane: "Well, after all those losses I'm due for a win."

Example #3:
Joe and Sam are at the race track betting on horses.

Joe: "You see that horse over there? He lost his last four races. I'm going to bet on him."
Sam: 'Why? I think he will probably lose."
Joe: "No way, Sam. I looked up the horse's stats and he has won half his races in the past two years. Since he has lost three of his last four races, he'll have to win this race. So I'm betting the farm on him."
Sam: "Are you sure?"
Joe: "Of course I'm sure. That pony is due, man…he's due!"

Genetic Fallacy

Description:
    A Genetic Fallacy is a line of "reasoning" in which a perceived defect in the origin of a claim or thing is taken to be evidence that discredits the claim or thing itself. It is also a line of reasoning in which the origin of a claim or thing is taken to be evidence for the claim or thing. This sort of "reasoning" has the following form:

1. The origin of a claim or thing is presented.
2. The claim is true (or false) or the thing is supported (or discredited).

    It is clear that sort of "reasoning" is fallacious. For example: "Bill claims that 1+1=2. However, my parents brought me up to believe that 1+1=254, so Bill must be wrong."

It should be noted that there are some cases in which the origin of a claim is relevant to the truth or falsity of the claim. For example, a claim that comes from a reliable expert is likely to be true (provided it is in her area of expertise).

Example #1:
"Yeah, the environmentalists do claim that over-development can lead to all kinds of serious problems. But we all know about those darn bunny huggers and their silly views!"

Example #2:
"I was brought up to believe in God, and my parents told me God exists, so He must."

Example #3:
"Sure, the media claims that Senator Bedfellow was taking kickbacks. But we all know about the media's credibility, don't we."

Guilt by Association

Also Known as: Bad Company Fallacy, Company that You Keep Fallacy
Description:

Guilt by Association is a fallacy in which a person rejects a claim simply because it is pointed out that people she dislikes accept the claim. This sort of "reasoning" has the following form:

1. It is pointed out that person A accepts claim P.
2. Therefore P is false

It is clear that sort of "reasoning" is fallacious. For example the following is obviously a case of poor "reasoning": "You think that 1+1=2. But, Adolf Hitler, Charles Manson, Joseph Stalin, and Ted Bundy all believed that 1+1=2. So, you shouldn't believe it."

The fallacy draws its power from the fact that people do not like to be associated with people they dislike. Hence, if it is shown that a person shares a belief with people he dislikes he might be influenced into rejecting that belief. In such cases the person will be rejecting the claim based on how he thinks or feels about the people who hold it and because he does not want to be associated with such people.

Of course, the fact that someone does not want to be associated with people she dislikes does not justify the rejection of any claim. For example, most wicked and terrible people accept that the earth revolves around the sun and that lead is heavier than helium. No sane person would reject these claims simply because this would put them in the company of people they dislike (or even hate).

Example #1:
Will and Kiteena are arguing over socialism. Kiteena is a pacifist and hates violence and violent people.

Kiteena: "I think that the United States should continue to adopt socialist programs. For example, I think that the government should take control of vital industries."
Will: "So, you are for state ownership of industry."
Kiteena: "Certainly. It is a great idea and will help make the world a less violent place."
Will: "Well, you know Stalin also endorsed state ownership on industry. At last count he wiped out millions of his own people. Pol Pot of Cambodia was also for state ownership of industry. He also killed millions of his own people. The leadership of China is for state owned industry. They killed their own people in that square. So, are you still for state ownership of industry?"
Kiteena: "Oh, no! I don't want to be associated with those butchers!"

Example #2:
Jen and Sandy are discussing the topic of welfare. Jen is fairly conservative politically but she has been an active opponent of racism. Sandy is extremely liberal politically.

Jen: "I was reading over some private studies of welfare and I think it would be better to have people work for their welfare. For example, people could pick up trash, put up signs, and maybe even do skilled labor that they are qualified for. This would probably make people feel better about themselves and it would get more out of our tax money."
Sandy: "I see. So, you want to have the poor people out on the streets picking up trash for their checks? Well, you know that is exactly the position David Count endorses."
Jen: "Who is he?"
Sandy: "I'm surprised you don't know him, seeing how alike you two are. He was a Grand Mooky Wizard for the Aryan Pure White League and is well known for his hatred of blacks and other minorities. With your views, you'd fit right in to his

little racist club."
Jen: "So, I should reject my view just because I share it with some racist?"
Sandy: "Of course."

Example #3:
Libard and Ferris are discussing who they are going to vote for as the next department chair in the philosophy department. Libard is a radical feminist and she despises Wayne and Bill, who are two sexist professors in the department.

Ferris: "So, who are you going to vote for?"
Libard: 'Well, I was thinking about voting for Jane, since she is a woman and there has never been a woman chair here. But, I think that Steve will do an excellent job. He has a lot of clout in the university and he is a decent person."
Ferris: "You know, Wayne and Bill are supporting him. They really like the idea of having Steve as the new chair. I never thought I'd see you and those two pigs on the same side."
Libard: "Well, maybe it is time that we have a woman as chair."

Hasty Generalization

Also Known as: Fallacy of Insufficient Statistics, Fallacy of Insufficient Sample, Leaping to a Conclusion, Hasty Induction
Description:
   This fallacy is committed when a person draws a conclusion about a population based on a sample that is not large enough. It has the following form:

1. Sample S, which is too small, is taken from population P.
2. Conclusion C is drawn about Population P based on S.

   The person committing the fallacy is misusing the following type of reasoning, which is known variously as Inductive Generalization, Generalization, and Statistical Generalization:

1. X% of all observed A's are B's.
2. Therefore X% of all A's are B's.

   The fallacy is committed when not enough A's are observed to warrant the conclusion. If enough A's are observed then the reasoning is not fallacious.
   Small samples will tend to be unrepresentative. As a blatant case, asking one

person what she thinks about gun control would clearly not provide an adequate sized sample for determining what Canadians in general think about the issue. The general idea is that small samples are less likely to contain numbers proportional to the whole population. For example, if a bucket contains blue, red, green and orange marbles, then a sample of three marbles cannot possible be representative of the whole population of marbles. As the sample size of marbles increases the more likely it becomes that marbles of each color will be selected in proportion to their numbers in the whole population. The same holds true for things others than marbles, such as people and their political views.

Since Hasty Generalization is committed when the sample (the observed instances) is too small, it is important to have samples that are large enough when making a generalization. The most reliable way to do this is to take as large a sample as is practical. There are no fixed numbers as to what counts as being large enough. If the population in question is not very diverse (a population of cloned mice, for example) then a very small sample would suffice. If the population is very diverse (people, for example) then a fairly large sample would be needed. The size of the sample also depends on the size of the population. Obviously, a very small population will not support a huge sample. Finally, the required size will depend on the purpose of the sample. If Bill wants to know what Joe and Jane think about gun control, then a sample consisting of Bill and Jane would (obviously) be large enough. If Bill wants to know what most Australians think about gun control, then a sample consisting of Bill and Jane would be far too small.

People often commit Hasty Generalizations because of bias or prejudice. For example, someone who is a sexist might conclude that all women are unfit to fly jet fighters because one woman crashed one. People also commonly commit Hasty Generalizations because of laziness or sloppiness. It is very easy to simply leap to a conclusion and much harder to gather an adequate sample and draw a justified conclusion. Thus, avoiding this fallacy requires minimizing the influence of bias and taking care to select a sample that is large enough.

One final point: a Hasty Generalization, like any fallacy, might have a true conclusion. However, as long as the reasoning is fallacious there is no reason to accept the conclusion based on that reasoning.

Example #1:
Smith, who is from England, decides to attend graduate school at Ohio State University. He has never been to the US before. The day after he arrives, he is walking back from an orientation session and sees two white (albino) squirrels chasing each other around a tree. In his next letter home, he tells his family that American squirrels are white.

Example #2:
Sam is riding her bike in her home town in Maine, minding her own business. A station wagon comes up behind her and the driver starts beeping his horn and then tries to force her off the road. As he goes by, the driver yells "get on the sidewalk where you belong!" Sam sees that the car has Ohio plates and concludes that all Ohio drivers are jerks.

Example #3:
Bill: "You know, those feminists all hate men."
Joe: "Really?"
Bill: "Yeah. I was in my philosophy class the other day and that Rachel chick gave a presentation."
Joe: "Which Rachel?"
Bill: "You know her. She's the one that runs that feminist group over at the Women's Center. She said that men are all sexist pigs. I asked her why she believed this and she said that her last few boyfriends were real sexist pigs."
Joe: "That doesn't sound like a good reason to believe that all of us are pigs."
Bill: "That was what I said."
Joe: "What did she say?"
Bill: "She said that she had seen enough of men to know we are all pigs. She obviously hates all men."
Joe: "So you think all feminists are like her?"
Bill: "Sure. They all hate men."

Historian's Fallacy

Also Known as: Hindsight Fallacy
Description:
   This fallacy, which is credited to David Hackett Fischer, occurs when it is assumed that people in the past viewed events with the same information or perspective as those analyzing these past events from a (relative) future. The fallacy has the following form:

1. From the present perspective event A in time T is seen as X (a good idea, significant, a bad idea, etc.)
2. Therefore event A was (or should have) been seen as X at time T.

   The X above can be many sorts of assessments, such as being a good idea, being of great significance, being a bad idea, being easily foreseeable, and so on.

This sort of reasoning is a fallacy because it is an error to infer that people in the past would (or should) see the events of their time from the perspective of those in their relative future. Obviously, the people in the past do not have the benefit of hindsight that those looking back possess.

It is not a fallacy to analyze past events from a present perspective, provided that the analysis is done in a way that attributes to those involved only the information they could reasonably be expected to have at the time. For example, suppose that Sally marries Bill and he seems fine until he becomes dangerously unstable. In this case, it would not be a fallacy to claim that it *turned out* to be a bad idea for Sally to marry Bill. It would be a fallacy to judge Sally as if she knew then what she only learned now. To use another example, if Sally did have adequate evidence that Bill was (or would become) dangerously unstable, then one would not commit this fallacy if one were to argue that she made a bad choice *when* she married him.

It also is not a fallacy to be critical of a person for what they reasonable should have known. For example, if Sally did not know about Bill being a psychopath because she married him a week after meeting him, it would be reasonable to argue that she made a poor choice in not getting to know more about him. This does not require having a perspective available only from the future and hence would not be fallacious.

Example #1
"It seems clear that Roosevelt must have known about the attack on Pearl Harbor and let it happen to ensure that we got into the war. After all, looking over all the historical data from the United States and Japan, the signs of an attack are so obvious. So, he surely must have known."

Example #2
Dan: "Did you hear? Kelly and Rob are getting divorced."
Lisa: "Why?"
Dan: "Well, Rob lost his job and…"
Lisa: "And she just dumped him as soon as she found out? Rob is such a great guy and I'm sure he'll get a new job. I set them up, you know!"
Dan: "No. He didn't tell her that he lost his job. He tried to find one, but he couldn't and it kind of broke him. He started drinking and he wrecked the car while driving drunk."
Lisa: "She should have known to never marry that loser!"

Illicit Conversion

Description:

This mistake occurs when someone makes illicit use of the conversion rule from categorical logic, which is a type of deductive logic.

In deductive logic, conversion is a rule that allows the subject and predicate claims of a categorical claim to be exchanged. As with most rules, it has correct and incorrect applications. In the case of conversion, the correctness of the application depends on what sort of claim is subjected to the rule.

In categorical logic there are four sentence types: *All S are P, No S are P, Some S are P*, and *Some S are not P*. C applies correctly to two of them: *No S are P* and *Some S are P*. A conversion is legitimate when the converted claim logically follows from the original (and vice versa). Put another way, the rule is applied correctly when its application does not change the truth value of the claim.

For example, "No cats are hamsters" converts legitimately to "no hamsters are cats." Interestingly, "some dogs are huskies" converts correctly to "some huskies are dogs", at least in categorical logic.

In categorical logic, "some" means "at least one." Hence, "at least one dog is a husky" is converted to "at least one husky is a dog." In this case, the inference from one to the other is legitimate because it is made in the context of categorical logic.

The illicit use of conversion is, not surprisingly, an error. This error occurs in two ways. The first is when the rule is applied incorrectly in the context of categorical logic: if conversion is applied to an *All S are P* or *Some S are not P* claim, then the rule has been applied improperly. This can be easily shown by the following examples.

The first example is that while it is true that all dogs are mammals, the conversion of this claim (that all mammals are dogs) is not true. As another example, the claim that some dogs are not huskies is true while its conversion (that some huskies are not dogs) is false. This sort of mistaken application of the conversion rule can also be presented as a fallacious line of reasoning, as shown by the following flawed inference patterns:

Fallacious Pattern #1
1. Premise: All S are P
2. Conclusion: All P are S

Fallacious Pattern #2
1. Premise: Some S are not P
2. Conclusion: Some P are not S

The second type of error occurs when the conversion rule is applied outside of the context of categorical logic as if it were being applied within such a context. To be specific, it occurs in contexts in which "some" does not mean "at least one." The mistake, which is sometimes known as an illicit inductive conversion, is as follows:

Fallacious Pattern #3
1. Premise: P% (or "some", "few", "most", "many", etc.) of Xs are Ys.
2. Conclusion: Therefore P% (or "some", etc.) of Ys are Xs.

For example, to infer that most people who speak English are from Maine because most people from Maine speak English would be an obvious error. This is because "most" in this context is not taken to mean "at least one" but is instead taken to refer to a majority.

Not surprisingly, people generally do not make such obvious errors in regards to conversion. However, people do fall victim to conversions that seem plausible. For example, when people hear that a medical test for a heart condition is 80% accurate they might be tempted to infer that 80% of those who test positive have the condition. However, to convert "80% of those who have the condition will test positive" (that is what it means for a test to be 80% accurate) to "80% of those who test positive have the condition" is an illicit use of conversion.

The following are examples of this sort of illicit conversion.

Example #1
"Very few white men have been President of the United States. Therefore very few Presidents have been white men."

Example #2
"A fairly small percentage of automobile accidents involve drivers over 70. Therefore a fairly small percentage of drivers over 70 are involved in automobile accidents."

Example#3
"Most conservatives are not media personalities on Fox News. Therefore, most of the media personalities on Fox News are not conservative."

Example #4
"Most wealthy people are men so most men are wealthy."

Example #5

"Most modern terrorists are Muslims, therefore most Muslims are modern terrorists."

Example #6

"Most modern terrorists are religious people, therefore most religious people are terrorists."

Ignoring a Common Cause

Also Known as: Questionable Cause
Description:
This fallacy has the following general structure:

1. A and B are regularly connected (but no third, common cause is looked for).
2. Therefore A is the cause of B.

This fallacy is committed when it is concluded that one thing causes another simply because they are regularly associated. More formally, this fallacy is committed when it is concluded that A is the cause of B simply because A and B are regularly connected. Further, the causal conclusion is drawn without considering the possibility that a third factor might be the cause of both A and B.

In many cases, the fallacy is quite evident. For example, if a person claimed that a person's sneezing was caused by her watery eyes and he simply ignored the fact that the woman was standing in a hay field, he would have fallen prey to the fallacy of ignoring a common cause. In this case, it would be reasonable to conclude that the woman's sneezing and watering eyes was caused by an allergic reaction of some kind. In other cases, it is not as evident that the fallacy is being committed. For example, a doctor might find a large amount of bacteria in one of her patients and conclude that the bacteria are the cause of the patient's illness. However, it might turn out that the bacteria are actually harmless and that a virus is weakening the person, Thus, the viruses would be the actual cause of the illness and growth of the bacteria (the viruses would weaken the ability of the person's body to resist the growth of the bacteria).

While causality is a rather difficult matter, this fallacy can be avoided by being be careful to check for other factors that might be the actual cause of both the suspected cause and the suspected effect. If a person fails to check for the possibility of a common cause, then they will commit this fallacy. Thus, it is always a good idea to always ask "could there be a third factor that is actually causing both A and B?"

Example #1:
One day Bill wakes up with a fever. A few hours later he finds that his muscles are sore. He concludes that the fever must have caused the soreness. His friend insists that the soreness and the fever are caused by some microbe. Bill laughs at this and insists that if he spends the day in a tub of cold water his soreness will go away.

Example #2:
Over the course of several weeks the leaves from the trees along the Wombat river fell into the water. Shortly thereafter, many dead fish were seen floating in the river. When the EPA investigated, the owners of the Wombat River Chemical Company claimed that is it was obvious that the leaves had killed the fish. Many local environmentalists claimed that the chemical plant's toxic wastes caused both the trees and the fish to die and that the leaves had no real effect on the fish.

Example #3:
A thunderstorm wakes Joe up in the middle of the night. He goes downstairs to get some milk to help him get back to sleep. On the way to the refrigerator, he notices that the barometer has fallen a great deal. Joe concludes that the storm caused the barometer to fall. In the morning he tells his wife about his conclusion. She tells him that it was a drop in atmospheric pressure that caused the barometer to drop and the storm.

Incomplete Evidence

Also Known As: Suppressed Evidence

This fallacy occurs when available evidence that would count against a conclusion is ignored or suppressed. It has the following form:

1. Evidence E is given for conclusion C.
2. Available evidence A that would count against C is ignored or suppressed.
3. Therefore, C is true.

Unlike many other fallacies, this fallacy does not arise because the presented premises fail to logically support the conclusion. Rather, the error is that the person making the argument fails (intentionally or accidentally) to take into account available evidence that is relevant to the truth of the conclusion. The fallacy does its work by conveying the impression to the target that the premises are both true and complete (that salient evidence has not been ignored or suppressed).

There are two factors that need to be considered as part of determining whether the fallacy has been committed or not.

The first is whether or not the suppressed/ignored evidence is actually significant enough to outweigh the presented evidence. The mere fact that some salient information has been left out is not enough to establish that the fallacy has been committed. What is needed is that the suppressed/ignored evidence is actually significant enough to make a difference. If not, the fallacy is not committed. It is also reasonable to consider whether or not the person was aware of the significance of the evidence. If not, then the person would not have intentionally committed the fallacy.

The second is that the (allegedly) suppressed/ignored evidence was reasonably available to the person committing the fallacy. If someone "ignored" evidence that he could not reasonably be expected to know, then he would not be committing this fallacy. Sorting out what a person can reasonably be expected to know can be a controversial matter in some cases, which is why there can be considerable dispute over specific cases alleged to involve this fallacy.

As a general guide, if the evidence was missed because of carelessness, bias, or lack of reasonable effort, then it would be reasonable to expect the person to be aware of the evidence in question. In any case, a person who knowingly suppresses or ignores evidence is clearly guilty of committing this fallacy.

One form of the fallacy of accent, namely quoting out of context, is also a type of incomplete evidence.

Example #1
"Most philosophers are men. Since Dr. Sarah Shute is a philosopher, Dr. Shute is a man."

Example #2
"People from the Middle East generally do not speak English fluently. So, I'll certainly need to get a translator when I interview the Israeli ambassador to the United States."

Example #3
Steve: "All those gun control laws are unconstitutional."
Mitt: "Could you be more specific?"
Steve: "Well, here is an example. By law, I can't bring my pistol to class."
Mitt: "How is that unconstitutional?"
Steve: "The Second Amendment clearly states that the right of the people to bear arms shall not be infringed. My right to bear my pistol in class is clearly being

infringed! So, that law is unconstitutional."

Mitt: "Maybe you should read the whole amendment and maybe some of the rulings on relevant cases. You are in law school, after all."

Example #4

David: "Did you read by blog about how the founding fathers were fundamentalist Christians?"

Thomas: "Not yet. Can you sum up your argument?"

David: "Sure. I went to the original texts and found all the references made to Christianity by the founding fathers that match fundamentalist ideas. I found quite a few and they clearly serve as evidence for my thesis. Those liberal atheists are really going to hate me!"

Thomas: "Hmm, that is interesting. But did you consider references they made to Christianity and other things that do not match your fundamentalism?"

David: "Well, no. My thesis is that they held to fundamentalist views. Why would I bother looking for evidence that they were not? I'm sure there isn't any."

Middle Ground

Also Known as: Golden Mean Fallacy, Fallacy of Moderation
Description:

This fallacy is committed when it is assumed that the middle position between two extremes must be correct simply because it is the middle position. this sort of "reasoning" has the following form:

1. Position A and B are two extreme positions.
2. C is a position that rests in the middle between A and B.
3. Therefore C is the correct position.

This line of "reasoning" is fallacious because it does not follow that a position is correct just because it lies in the middle of two extremes. This is shown by the following example. Suppose that a person is selling his computer. He wants to sell it for the current market value, which is $800 and someone offers him $1 for it. It would hardly follow that $400.50 is the proper price.

This fallacy draws its power from the fact that a moderate or middle position is often the correct one. For example, a moderate amount of exercise is better than too much exercise or too little exercise. However, this is not simply because it lies in the middle ground between two extremes. It is because too much exercise is harmful and too little exercise is all but useless. The basic idea behind many cases in which moderation is correct is that the extremes are typically "too much" and "not enough" and the middle position is "enough." In such cases the middle position is correct almost by definition.

It should be kept in mind that while uncritically assuming that the middle position must be correct because it is the middle position is poor reasoning it does not follow that accepting a middle position is always fallacious. As was just mentioned, many times a moderate position is correct. However, the claim that the moderate or middle position is correct must be supported by legitimate reasoning.

Example #1:
Some people claim that God is all powerful, all knowing, and all good. Other people claim that God does not exist at all. Now, it seems reasonable to accept a position somewhere in the middle. So, it is likely that God exists, but that he is only very powerful, very knowing, and very good. That seems right to me.

Example #2:
Congressman Jones has proposed cutting welfare payments by 50% while Congresswoman Shender has proposed increasing welfare payments by 10% to keep up with inflation and cost of living increases. I think that the best proposal is the one made by Congressman Trumple. He says that a 30% decrease in welfare payments is a good middle ground, so I think that is what we should support.

Example #3:
A month ago, a tree in Bill's yard was damaged in a storm. His neighbor, Joe, asked him to have the tree cut down so it would not fall on Joe's new shed. Bill refused to do this. Two days later another storm blew the tree onto Joe's new shed. Joe demanded that Joe pay the cost of repairs, which was $250. Bill said that he wasn't going to pay a cent. Obviously, the best solution is to reach a compromise between the two extremes, so Bill should pay Joe $125.

Misleading Vividness

Description:
Misleading Vividness is a fallacy in which a very small number of particularly dramatic events are taken to outweigh a significant amount of statistical evidence. This sort of "reasoning" has the following form:

1. Dramatic or vivid event X occurs (and is not in accord with the majority of the statistical evidence).

2. Therefore events of type X are likely to occur.

This sort of "reasoning" is fallacious because the mere fact that an event is particularly vivid or dramatic does not make the event more likely to occur, especially in the face of significant statistical evidence.

People often accept this sort of "reasoning" because particularly vivid or dramatic cases tend to make a very strong impression on the human mind. For example, if a person survives a particularly awful plane crash, he might be inclined to believe that air travel is more dangerous than other forms of travel. After all, explosions and people dying around him will have a more significant impact on his mind than will the rather dull statistics that a person is more likely to be struck by lightning than killed in a plane crash.

It should be kept in mind that taking into account the possibility of something dramatic or vivid occurring is not always fallacious. For example, a person might decide to never go sky diving because the effects of an accident can be very, very dramatic. If he knows that, statistically, the chances of the accident are happening are very low but he considers even a small risk to be unacceptable, then he would not be making an error in reasoning.

Example #1:
Bill and Jane are talking about buying a computer.

Jane: "I've been thinking about getting a computer. I'm really tired of having to wait in the library to write my papers."
Bill: 'What sort of computer do you want to get?"
Jane: "Well, it has to be easy to use, have a low price and have decent processing power. I've been thinking about getting a Kiwi Fruit 2200. I read in that consumer magazine that they have been found to be very reliable in six independent industry studies."
Bill: "I wouldn't get the Kiwi Fruit. A friend of mine bought one a month ago to finish his master's thesis. He was halfway through it when smoke started pouring out of the CPU. He didn't get his thesis done on time and he lost his financial aid. Now he's working over at the Gut Boy Burger Warehouse."
Jane: "I guess I won't go with the Kiwi!"

Example #2:
Joe and Drew are talking about flying.
Joe: "When I was flying back to school, the pilot came on the intercom and told us that the plane was having engine trouble. I looked out the window and I saw smoke billowing out of the engine nearest me. We had to make an emergency landing and there were fire trucks everywhere. I had to spend the next six hours sitting in the airport waiting for a flight. I was lucky I didn't die! I'm never flying again."
Drew: "So how are you going to get home over Christmas break?"
Joe: "I'm going to drive. That will be a lot safer than flying."
Drew: "I don't think so. You are much more likely to get injured or killed driving than flying."
Joe: "I don't buy that! You should have seen the smoke pouring out of that engine! I'm never getting on one of those death traps again!"

Example #3:
Jane and Sarah are talking about running in a nearby park.

Jane: "Did you hear about that woman who was attacked in Tuttle Park?"
Sarah: "Yes. It was terrible."
Jane: "Don't you run there every day?"
Sarah: "Yes."
Jane: 'How can you do that? I'd never be able to run there!"
Sarah: "Well, as callous as this might sound, that attack was out of the ordinary. I've been running there for three years and this has been the only attack. Sure, I worry about being attacked, but I'm not going give up my running just because there is some slight chance I'll be attacked."
Sarah: "That is stupid! I'd stay away from that park if I was you! That woman was really beat up badly so you know it is going to happen again. If you don't stay out of that park, it will happen to you!"

Moving the Goal Posts

Also Known As: Raising the Bar
Description:

This fallacy occurs when evidence against a claim is rejected by insisting, in an unprincipled way, that different (typically greater) evidence be provided. The fallacy has the following form:

1. Evidence E against claim C is presented.
2. It is insisted (without justification) that a different sort of evidence, D, must be presented.
3. E is rejected.
4. C is true (optional).

This is a fallacy because changing the conditions under which something counts as evidence against a claim (in an unprincipled way) does not show that the evidence does not count against the claim. This is analogous to moving a goal post after a goal has been scored and then insisting that the goal does not count.

It is not a fallacy to argue that alleged evidence against a claim is not, in fact, evidence against a claim. The fallacy occurs when the rejection of the evidence is done in a way that is not justified (typically this is done simply to "protect" the claim from criticism). There are cases in which the standards of what count as evidence against a claim can be shifted during the course of an argument. However, this must be done in a manner that is adequately justified. Not surprisingly, what counts as a justified change in standards can be a matter of considerable debate and goes beyond the scope of this book.

There is also another version of this fallacy in which a claim is "defended" from refutation by switching to a new or modified claim and treating that claim as if it were the original claim.

Example #1
Gary: "The moon landings were faked. If they were real, there would be photos of the landing sites from later probes."
Janet: "Well, there are. NASA released the photos a while ago."
Gary: "Well, NASA no doubt modified the images using Photoshop."
Janet: "That kind of modification can be checked, you know."
Gary: "NASA's technology is really good. They can fool the experts."
Janet: "Well, what about the Russians. If we had faked the landings, they would have revealed it to the world."
Gary: "The Russians were in on it. We lied for them, they lie for us."
Janet: "For the love of God, what would count as proof? What if you were able to go to the moon and see the lander?"
Gary: "That could be planted there before I arrive."
Janet: "I give up."
Gary: "I win!"

Example #2

Donald: "I still have doubts that Obama was born in America."

Bill: "I didn't vote for him, but he released his certificate of live birth. That seems good enough for me."

Donald: "But a certificate of live birth is not the same thing as a birth certificate, so I have my doubts."

Bill: "Legally, it is good enough. Also, do you think that McCain, Rove, and all those major Republicans wouldn't have challenged him if there was any basis for this?"

Donald: "They're politicians, so they all stick together."

Bill: "Yeah, I can see the love they have for Obama. But, it doesn't really matter-Obama released his 'long form" birth certificate, you know."

Donald: "That could be a fake."

Example #3

Rachel: "I'm not getting my son vaccinated. They cause autism."

Juan: "That does not seem to be true."

Rachel: "It is. The mercury in the thimerosal used as preservative for vaccines causes autism."

Juan: "Well, that was removed from vaccines years ago and there was no statistically significant change."

Rachel: "Well, the toxins in the vaccines cause autism."

Juan: "This has been thoroughly investigated and no causal link has been found. But don't take my word on this-check out the studies."

Rachel: "Those studies are flawed. No doubt they were sponsored by the companies that sell vaccines."

Oversimplified Cause

Description:

This fallacy occurs when someone infers that only one cause is responsible for an effect and the person fails to consider that there might be multiple causes. This fallacy has the following form:

1. Effect E occurs
2. Therefore, C is the *single* cause of E.

This is an error in reasoning because the possibility of multiple causes should be considered when engaging in causal reasoning. This fallacy often occurs because sorting out complicated casual situations can be difficult and it is far easier to simply focus on one alleged cause.

In some cases, people commit this fallacy in ignorance-that is, they simple fail to consider that the causal situation might be complicated rather than simple. In other cases, this fallacy is used intentionally in an attempt to get people to accept that there is a single cause. This is sometimes done for political reasons and, not surprisingly, the single cause focused on tends to nicely fit in with the person's political agenda.

It is important to note that this error can still be committed when there really is only a single cause, provided that the person making the error fails to even consider the possibility that there are multiple causes. Naturally, some situations might so obviously be cases of a single cause that only the most minimal effort is required to eliminate the possibility of multiple causes.

Example #1
Rick: "It looks like our schools are in rough shape. I saw that Americans are lagging way behind the rest of the world in areas like math and science."
Ed: "Yup. It is those damn teacher unions. They ruined education. If we could just rid of the unions, we'd be on top of the world again."

Example #2
"The recent economic meltdown was an incredible financial disaster. However, nothing has been done to address its cause, namely allowing mortgage companies to make subprime loans."

Overconfident Inference from Unknown Statistics

Description:
This fallacy is committed when a person places unwarranted confidence in drawing a conclusion from statistics that are unknown.

1. "Unknown" statistical data D is presented.
2. Conclusion C is drawn from D with greater confidence than D warrants.

Unknown statistical data is just that, statistical data that is unknown. This data is different from "data" that is simply made up because it has at least some foundation.

One common type of unknown statistical data is when educated guesses are made based on limited available data. For example, when experts estimate the number of people who use illegal drugs, they are making an educated guess. As another example, when the number of total deaths in the Iraqi war is reported, it is (at best) an educated guess because no one knows for sure how many people have been killed.

Another common type of unknown statistical date is when the data can only be gathered in ways that are likely to result in incomplete or inaccurate data. For example, statistical data about the number of people who have affairs is likely to be in this category.

Obviously, unknown statistical data is not very good data. However, drawing an inference from such data is not, in itself, an error. In some cases, such inferences can be quite reasonable.

For example, while the exact number of people killed in the Iraq war is unknown, it is reasonable to infer from the data that many people have died. As another example, while the exact number of people who do not pay their taxes is unknown, it is reasonable to infer that the government is losing some revenue because of this.

The error that makes this a fallacy is to place too much confidence in a conclusion drawn from such unknown data. Or, to be a bit more technical, to overestimate the strength of the argument based on statistical data that is not adequately known.

This is an error because, obviously enough, a conclusion is being drawn that is not adequately justified by the premises.

Naturally, the way in which the statistical data is gathered also needs to be assessed to determine whether or not other errors have occurred.

Example #1
"Several American Muslims are known to be terrorists or at least terrorist supporters. As such, I estimate that there are hundreds of actual and thousands of potential Muslim-American terrorists. Based on this, I am certain that we are in grave danger from this large number of enemies within our own borders."

Example #2
"Experts estimate that there are about 11 million illegal immigrants in the United States. While some people are not worried about this, consider the fact that the experts estimate that illegals make up about 5% of the total work force. This definitely explains that percentage of American unemployment since these illegals are certainly stealing 5% of America's jobs."

Example #3

Sally: "I just read an article about cheating."

Jane: "How to do it?"

Sally: "No! It was about the number of men who cheat."

Sasha: "So, what did it say?"

Sally: "Well, the author estimated that 40% of men cheat."

Kelly: "Hmm, there are five of us here."

Janet: "You know what that means…"

Sally: "Yes, two of our boyfriends are cheating on us. I always thought Bill and Sam had that look…"

Janet: "Hey! Bill would never cheat on me! I bet it is your man-he is always given me the eye!"

Sally: 'What! I'll kill him!"

Janet: "Calm down. I was just kidding. I mean, how can they know that 40% of men cheat? I'm sure none of the boys are cheating on us. Well, except maybe Sally's man."

Sally: "Hey!"

Pathetic Fallacy

Also Known As: Anthropomorphic Fallacy, Personification Fallacy

Description:

This fallacy occurs when inanimate objects are treated as if they possessed mental states such as feelings, thoughts, sensations, and motivations. In order to be a fallacy in the technical sense, a conclusion must be drawn on the basis of this assumption. However, by popular usage the "fallacy" occurs simply from treating an inanimate object in this way. As a fallacy in the strict sense it has the following form:

1. Inanimate object (or force) O is treated as if it had mental state M.
2. O was involved in event E.
3. Therefore, O's role in E is due to M.

This is an error because it attributes to inanimate objects animate qualities, which they do not (by definition) possess, and uses this attribution to support a conclusion. As an actual fallacy in the technical sense, it is actually fairly rare.

Far more commonly the pathetic fallacy is taken to include cases in which no conclusion is drawn. For example, if someone says "the sea is angry" and leaves it at that, then there would be no fallacy in the strict sense of the term. However, this would be regarded as the pathetic fallacy in the popular use of the term.

The pathetic fallacy is also taken as occurring in cases involving explanations that are flawed because they involve attributing mental states to inanimate forces or objects. For example: "When it gets hot, air wants to rise." Since air has no wants, this would be an inadequate explanation.

This fallacy derives its name from "pathos" rather than "pathetic" in the pejorative sense.

Example #1
"I was working on my paper and the darn computer crashed. That computer never liked me, so I must infer that it did that out of spite."

Example #2
Les: "Thanks for letting me borrow your car, but it won't start."
Mel: "She is very temperamental. Did you try sweet talking her?"
Les: "Um, no. I did check the battery, though."
Mel: "Here, I'll give it a try."
Les: "Okay."
Mel: "Good morning Lucile! How about going for a trip with Les?"
Lucile: "Vrooom!"
Mel: "You see, this shows that she has to be sweet talked into starting."
Les: "Thanks again. I'll be sure to talk nicely to her there and back!"

Peer Pressure

Description:
Peer Pressure is a fallacy in which a threat of rejection by one's peers (or peer pressure) is substituted for evidence in an "argument." This line of "reasoning" has the following form:

1. Person P is pressured by his/her peers or threatened with rejection.
2. Therefore person P's claim X is false.

This line of "reasoning" is fallacious because peer pressure and threat of rejection do not constitute evidence for rejecting a claim. This is especially clear in the following example:

Joe: "Bill, I know you think that 1+1=2. But we don't accept that sort of thing in our group."

Bill: "I was just joking. Of course I don't believe that."

It is clear that the pressure from Bill's group has no bearing on the truth of the claim that 1+1=2.

It should be noted that loyalty to a group and the need to belong can give people very strong reasons to conform to the views and positions of those groups. Further, from a practical standpoint we must often compromise our beliefs in order to belong to groups. However, this feeling of loyalty or the need to belong simply do not constitute evidence for a claim.

Example #1:
Bill says that he likes the idea that people should work for their welfare when they can. His friends laugh at him, accuse him of fascist leanings, and threaten to ostracize him from their group. He decides to recant and abandon his position to avoid rejection.

Example #2:
Bill: "I like classical music and I think it is of higher quality than most modern music."
Jill: "That stuff is for old people."
Dave: "Yeah, only real sissy monkeys listen to that crap. Besides, Anthrax rules! It Rules!"
Bill: "Well, I don't really like it that much. Anthrax is much better."

Example #3:
Bill thinks that welfare is needed in some cases. His friends in the Young Republicans taunt him every time he makes his views known. He accepts their views in order to avoid rejection.

Personal Attack

Also Known as: Ad Hominem Abusive
Description:
A personal attack is committed when a person substitutes abusive remarks for evidence when attacking another person's claim or claims. This line of "reasoning" is fallacious because the attack is directed at the person making the claim and not the claim itself. The truth value of a claim is independent of the person making the claim. After all, no matter how repugnant an individual might be, he or she can

still make true claims.

Not all ad Hominems are fallacious. In some cases, an individual's characteristics can have a bearing on the question of the veracity of her claims. For example, if someone is shown to be a pathological liar, then what he says can be considered to be unreliable. However, such attacks are weak, since even pathological liars might speak the truth on occasion.

In general, it is best to focus one's attention on the content of the claim and not on who made the claim. It is the content that determines the truth of the claim and not the characteristics of the person making the claim.

Example #1:
In a school debate, Bill claims that the President's economic plan is unrealistic. His opponent, a professor, retorts by saying "the freshman has his facts wrong."

Example #2:
"This theory about a potential cure for cancer has been introduced by a doctor who is a known lesbian feminist. I don't see why we should extend an invitation for her to speak at the World Conference on Cancer."

Example #3:
"Bill says that we should give tax breaks to companies. But he is untrustworthy, so it must be wrong to do that."

Example #4:
"That claim cannot be true. Dave believes it, and we know how morally repulsive he is."

Example #5:
"Bill claims that Jane would be a good treasurer. However I find Bill's behavior offensive, so I'm not going to vote for Jill."

Example #6
"Jane says that drug use is morally wrong, but she is just a goody-two shoes Christian, so we don't have to listen to her."

Example #7
Bill: "I don't think it is a good idea to cut social programs."
Jill: "Why not?"
Bill: "Well, many people do not get a fair start in life and hence need some help.

After all, some people have wealthy parents and have it fairly easy. Others are born into poverty and…"

Jill: "You just say that stuff because you have a soft heart and an equally soft head."

Poisoning the Well

Description:

This sort of "reasoning" involves trying to discredit what a person might later claim by presenting unfavorable information (be it true or false) about the person. This "argument" has the following form:

1. Unfavorable information (be it true or false) about person A is presented.
2. Therefore any claims person A makes will be false.

This sort of "reasoning" is obviously fallacious. The person making such an attack is hoping that the unfavorable information will bias listeners against the person in question and hence that they will reject any claims he might make. However, merely presenting unfavorable information about a person (even if it is true) hardly counts as evidence against the claims he/she might make. This is especially clear when Poisoning the Well is looked at as a form of ad Hominem in which the attack is made prior to the person even making the claim or claims. The following example clearly shows that this sort of "reasoning" is quite poor.

Example #1:
"Don't listen to him, he's a scoundrel."

Example #2:
"Before turning the floor over to my opponent, I ask you to remember that those who oppose my plans do not have the best wishes of the university at heart."

Example #3:
You are told, prior to meeting him, that your friend's boyfriend is a decadent wastrel. When you meet him, everything you hear him say is tainted.

Example #4
Before class
Bill: "Boy, that professor is a real jerk. I think he is some sort of Eurocentric fascist."
Jill: "Yeah."

During Class:
Prof. Jones: "...and so we see that there was never any 'Golden Age of Matriarchy' in 1895 in America."
After Class:
Bill: "See what I mean?"
Jill: "Yeah. There must have been a Golden Age of Matriarchy, since that jerk said there wasn't."

Positive Ad Hominem

Description:

Translated from Latin to English, "ad Hominem" means "against the man" or "against the person." The positive ad homimen can be seen as a "reverse" ad hominem. A "standard" ad homimem is a fallacy in which a claim is rejected on the basis of some irrelevant fact about the author of or the person presenting the claim. A positive ad hominem occurs when a claim is accepted on the basis of some irrelevant fact about the author or person presenting the claim or argument. Typically, this fallacy involves two steps. First, something positive (but irrelevant) about the character of person making the claim, her circumstances, or her actions is made. Second, this is taken to be evidence for the claim in question. This fallacy has the following form:

1. Person A makes claim X.
2. Person B notes a positive (but logically irrelevant) feature of A.
3. Therefore A's claim is true.

The reason why an ad Hominem (of any kind) is a fallacy is that the character, circumstances, or actions of a person do not (in most cases) have a bearing on the truth or falsity of the claim being made. There are cases in which facts about a person can be relevant to assessing that person's credibility and there are also cases in which non-fallacious arguments can be made based on a person's expertise (as per the Argument from Authority). For example, it would not be a fallacy to accept an expert's claim in her field because she is well educated in the field, unbiased, and experienced in the field.

Example #1
"That Glenn is such a nice man and always so passionate about what he says. So, he must be right that we should buy gold."

Example #2

Sally: "What he said was ridiculous. Why do believe him?"

Janet: "Honey, with a butt like that, how can he be wrong?"

Sally: "Well, he was certainly talking out of it."

Example #3

"I had some doubts about him, but then I realized that he was wearing an expensive suit. Plus, he had that British accent. There is no way he could be lying about this deal, so I am sure it will be a great investment!"

Post Hoc

Also Known as: Post Hoc Ergo Propter Hoc, False Cause, Questionable Cause, Confusing Coincidental Relationships With Causes

Description:

A Post Hoc is a fallacy with the following form:

1. A occurs before B.
2. Therefore A is the cause of B.

The Post Hoc fallacy derives its name from the Latin phrase "Post hoc, ergo propter hoc." This has been traditionally interpreted as "After this, therefore because of this." This fallacy is committed when it is concluded that one event causes another simply because the proposed cause occurred before the proposed effect. More formally, the fallacy involves concluding that A causes or caused B because A occurs before B and there is not sufficient evidence to actually warrant such a claim.

It is evident in many cases that the mere fact that A occurs before B in no way indicates a causal relationship. For example, suppose Jill, who is in London, sneezed at the exact same time an earthquake started in California. It would clearly be irrational to arrest Jill for starting a natural disaster, since there is no reason to suspect any causal connection between the two events. While such cases are quite obvious, the Post Hoc fallacy is fairly common because there are cases in which there might be some connection between the events. For example, a person who has her computer crash after she installs a new piece of software would probably suspect that the software was to blame. If she simply concluded that the software caused the crash because it was installed before the crash she would be committing the Post Hoc fallacy. In such cases the fallacy would be committed because the evidence provided fails to justify acceptance of the causal claim. It is even theoretically possible for the fallacy to be committed when A really does cause B, provided that the "evidence" given consists only of the claim that A occurred before B. The key to the Post Hoc fallacy is not that there is no causal connection between A and B. It is that adequate evidence has not been provided for a claim that A causes B. Thus, Post Hoc resembles a Hasty Generalization in that it involves making a leap to an unwarranted conclusion. In the case of the Post Hoc fallacy, that leap is to a causal claim instead of a general proposition.

Not surprisingly, many superstitions are probably based on Post Hoc reasoning. For example, suppose a person buys a good luck charm, does well on his exam, and then concludes that the good luck charm caused him to do well. This person would have fallen victim to the Post Hoc fallacy. This is not to say that all "superstitions" have no basis at all. For example, some "folk cures" have actually been found to work.

Post Hoc fallacies are typically committed because people are simply not careful enough when they reason. Leaping to a causal conclusion is always easier and faster than actually investigating the phenomenon. However, such leaps tend to land far from the truth of the matter. Because Post Hoc fallacies are committed by drawing an unjustified causal conclusion, the key to avoiding them is careful investigation. While it is true that causes precede effects (outside of Star Trek, anyway), it is not true that precedence makes something a cause of something else. Because of this, a causal investigation should begin with finding what occurs before the effect in question, but it should not end there.

Example #1:
I had been doing pretty poorly this season. Then my girlfriend gave me this neon laces for my spikes and I won my next three races. Those laces must be good luck…if I keep on wearing them I can't help but win!

Example #2:
Bill purchases a new PowerMac and it works fine for months. He then buys and installs a new piece of software. The next time he starts up his Mac, it freezes. Bill concludes that the software must be the cause of the freeze.

Example #3:
Joan is scratched by a cat while visiting her friend. Two days later she comes down with a fever. Joan concludes that the cat's scratch must be the cause of her illness.

Example #4:
The Republicans pass a new tax reform law that benefits wealthy Americans. Shortly thereafter the economy takes a nose dive. The Democrats claim that the tax reform caused the economic woes and they push to get rid of it.

Example #5:
The picture on Jim's old TV set goes out of focus. Jim goes over and strikes the TV soundly on the side and the picture goes back into focus. Jim tells his friend that hitting the TV fixed it.

Example #6:
Jane gets a rather large wart on her finger. Based on a story her father told her, she cuts a potato in half, rubs it on the wart and then buries it under the light of a full moon. Over the next month her wart shrinks and eventually vanishes. Jane writes her father to tell him how right he was about the cure.

Proving X, Concluding Y

Also Known As: Missing the Point, Irrelevant Thesis
Description:
This fallacy occurs when a conclusion is drawn from evidence that does not actually support that conclusion but does support another claim. The form of this reasoning is as follows:

1. Evidence E for claim X is presented.
2. Therefore Y

While all fallacies are such that the alleged evidence provided in the premise(s) fails to adequately support the conclusion, what distinguishes this fallacy is that the evidence presented actually does provide support for a claim. However, it does not support the conclusion that is actually presented.

This fallacy typically occurs when the evidence for X seems vaguely connected or vaguely relevant to Y in a logical way, but actually is not. It is this seeming relevance or connection that lures the victim into accepting the conclusion. The victim of the fallacy can also be the person committing the fallacy.

A person can commit this fallacy and be aware the conclusion does not follow from the evidence. In such cases, the person typically makes use of the apparent logical connection between the evidence and the conclusion to mislead someone into accepting it. This could, perhaps, be called "the bait and switch fallacy."

Obviously, this fallacy (like all fallacies) is a case of non-sequiter ("does not follow") in which the conclusion does not logically follow from the premises. However, this specific sort of mistake is common and interesting enough to justify giving it its own name and entry.

Example #1
"I am troubled by the reports of binge drinking by college students. According to the statistics I have seen, about 19% of college students are binge drinkers and this leads to problems ranging from poor academic performance to unplanned pregnancies. Since people often drink in response to pressure, this shows that professors are putting their students under too much pressure and hence need to make their classes easier."

Example #2
"Our product testing revealed that 60% of the people on Acme Diet Master reported that they felt less hungry when using the product. This shows that 60% ate less when using our product. I think we have our next big product!"

Example #3
"High tax rates for individuals leave them with far less money to spend. High tax rates for business often leads them to lower salaries, which means people have far less money to spend. In these troubled economic times, revitalizing the economy requires that Americans spend more. Therefore, the obvious solution is to abolish all taxes."

Psychologist's fallacy

Description:
This fallacy occurs when it is concluded that another person has a certain mental quality (or qualities) because the person drawing that conclusion has that quality (or qualities). This fallacy has the following form:

1. Person A has mental quality (or qualities) Q (a belief, a skill, knowledge, or tendency to act a certain way, etc.).
2. Person A concludes that person B has Q a well.

The error being made is essentially that of a weak analogy: person A is drawing a conclusion about person B based on an unsupported assumption that A and B are alike. Without adequate reason to think that A and B are alike enough in relevant ways, concluding that they are alike in regards to the quality in question would be unjustified.

This fallacy can be avoided by making an adequate argument from analogy. This would involve providing the key premises establishing that A and B are alike in ways relevant to the quality in question.

The fallacy received its name from William James who noted that psychologists are particularly prone to ascribing their own standpoints to those they examine. A person does not, of course, need to be a professional psychologist to commit this fallacy.

Example #1

Christine: "Thanks for coming to dinner! I made bacon burgers. With cheese!"
Florence: "Why?"
Christine: "I really like them. I figured you would, too."
Florence: "I'm a vegetarian. Do you have anything I can eat?"
Christine: "Well, you can put the cheese, lettuce and onions on the bun."
Florence: "I don't like onions. Or lettuce."

Example #2

"I'm sure those people will help me push my car out of the ditch. After all, I'd help out someone who is in the same predicament."

Example #3

Bob: "Did you hear that the legislature just voted on a law legalizing same sex marriage?"
Gretchen: "No way!"
Bob: "Really. It is going to the governor."
Gretchen: "There is no way she'll sign it!"
Bob: "Really? Why?"
Gretchen: "Well, I wouldn't! So I'm sure she won't!"
Bob: 'Uh, huh. Well, would you have voted for the law if you were in the house or state senate?"
Gretchen: "Hell no!"
Bob: "And yet the bill passed…"

Example #4

Bill: "I'm sure that no one would like that movie."
Paul: "Why?"
Bill: "Well, I did not like it."

Questionable Cause

Description:

This fallacy has the following general form:

1. A and B are associated on a regular basis.
2. Therefore A is the cause of B.

The general idea behind this fallacy is that it is an error in reasoning to conclude that one thing causes another simply because the two are associated on a regular basis. More formally, this fallacy is committed when it is concluded that A is the cause of B simply because they are associated on a regular basis. The error being made is that a causal conclusion is being drawn from inadequate evidence.

The Questionable Cause Fallacy is actually a general type of fallacy. Any causal fallacy that involves an error in a reasoning due to a failure to adequately investigate the suspected cause is a fallacy of this type. Thus, fallacies like Post Hoc and Confusing Cause and Effect are specific examples of the general Questionable Cause Fallacy.

Causal reasoning can be quite difficult since causation is a rather complex philosophic issue. The complexity of causation is briefly discussed in the context of the specific versions of this fallacy.

The key to avoiding the Questionable Cause fallacy is to take due care in drawing causal conclusions. This requires taking steps to adequately investigate the phenomena in question as well using the proper methods of careful investigation.

Example #1:

Joe gets a chain letter that threatens him with dire consequences if he breaks the chain. He laughs at it and throws it in the garbage. On his way to work he slips and breaks his leg. When he gets back from the hospital he sends out 200 copies of the chain letter, hoping to avoid further accidents.

Example #2:

When investigating a pond students found a severe drop in the fish population. Further investigation revealed the fishes' food supply had been severely reduced. At first the students believed the lack of food was killing the fish, but then they realized they had to find what was causing the decline in the food supply. The students suspected acid rain was the cause of both the reduction in the fish population and food supply. However, the local business council insisted it was the lack of food that reduced the fish population. Most of the townspeople agreed with this conclusion since it seemed obvious a lack of food would cause fish to die

Rationalization

Description:

Rationalization occurs when a person offers a reason (or reasons) in support of a claim when this reason is not the person's actual reason for accepting the claim.

1. A reason, R1, is presented by person P for claim C.
2. But, P's real reason for accepting C is R2.
3. P accepts C on the basis of R1.

While people can aid others in rationalizing, this fallacy is often self-inflicted. In such cases a person engages in self-deception about the true reason (or reasons) for accepting the claim. This fallacy can, of course, be used to mislead others. The most common use is when a person presents a laudable reason to justify an action when the person's actual motivation would not sound as good to others.

What distinguishes rationalization from outright lying is that rationalization is generally taken as requiring an element of actual self-deception. That is, the person rationalizing tends to accept, at least on some level, the professed reason as being the actual reason.

Determining when a person is rationalizing can be rather challenging. After all, this requires having grounds to believe that the reason being given is not the actual reason and that the person is engaged, at least in some degree, in self-deception.

When people rationalize, they often find it difficult to accept that they are doing so. After all, they will be putting effort into convincing themselves that their actual reason is their professed reason. While it can be difficult, it is wise to be on guard against this tendency to avoid deceiving yourself.

Some people define "rationalization" in a way that does not require self-deception but merely the presentation of a reason that is not the person's actual reason. In this case, showing that a person is rationalizing does not require showing that self-deception is involved. All that is needed is evidence that the actual and professed reasons are not the same.

Example #1
Rick: "Man, gas prices are going up."
Mick: "They sure are. I've been driving less."
Rick: "I'm going to buy a motorcycle. They get excellent gas mileage. I'll save a lot of money."
Mick: "Good idea. Are you selling your car?"
Rick: "Well, no. I'll need it when the weather is bad and to transport stuff."
Mick: "Makes sense. So, what kind are you getting? Since you are trying to save

money, I assume you'll be getting the least expensive bike."

Rick: "This is the one I'm looking at."

Mick: "Hmm, that is a $25,000 sports bike."

Rick: "It gets better mileage than my car. I'll save a ton of money on gas."

Mick: "But it is $25,000..."

Rick: "Look at this-that is the helmet I ordered. I also got a full racing grade riding suit and these top grade leather boots. The motorcycle trailer is on back order, but it should get here in two weeks."

Mick: "You'll sure save a lot of money with all that stuff."

Rick: "Yup. See, here is the gas mileage for the bike. Way better than my car. Heck, it is even better than a Prius."

Mick: "Hey, you could buy one of those and save even more money."

Rick: "A Prius? Seriously? I might as well get neutered."

Example #2

Jack: "Happy birthday! I got you the new Zbox 720 and an HD TV!"

Cynthia: "But I don't play video games. You do. But the TV is nice. I can put it in my workout room."

Jack: "Um, the TV is for the Zbox."

Cynthia: "Um, why would you be playing your Zbox in my workout room?"

Jack: 'I won't. The TV and the Zbox are for my man cave."

Cynthia: "How is this a present for me?"

Jack: "Well, you are always complaining that I am playing my video games when you want to watch TV. This way you get a great gift: I'll be in my man cave playing my Zbox 720 on the HD TV while you are watching TV."

Cynthia: "My, this is the best present ever."

Jack: "I know! I just knew that this would be the best gift for your birthday!"

Red Herring

Also Known as: Smoke Screen, Wild Goose Chase

Description:

A Red Herring is a fallacy in which an irrelevant topic is presented in order to divert attention from the original issue. The basic idea is to "win" an argument by leading attention away from the argument and to another topic. This sort of "reasoning" has the following form:

1. Topic A is under discussion.
2. Topic B is introduced under the guise of being relevant to topic A (when topic B is actually not relevant to topic A).
3. Topic A is abandoned.

 This sort of "reasoning" is fallacious because merely changing the topic of discussion hardly counts as an argument against a claim.

Example #1:
"Argument" against a bond measure:

"We admit that this measure is popular. But we also urge you to note that there are so many bond issues on this ballot that the whole thing is getting ridiculous."

Example #2:
"Argument" for a tax cut:

"You know, I've begun to think that there is some merit in the Republicans' tax cut plan. I suggest that you come up with something like it, because If we Democrats are going to survive as a party, we have got to show that we are as tough-minded as the Republicans, since that is what the public wants."

Example #3:
"Argument" for making grad school requirements stricter:
"I think there is great merit in making the requirements stricter for the graduate students. I recommend that you support it, too. After all, we are in a budget crisis and we do not want our salaries affected."

Reification, Fallacy of

Also Known As: Fallacy of Hypostatisation
Description:
 This fallacy occurs when an abstraction is assumed to be a real, concrete entity and a conclusion is drawn from this assumption. The fallacy has the following form:

1. Abstraction A is treated as if it were a real, concrete entity.
2. Treating A as real is taken to entail C.
3. Therefore, C is true.

The mistake being made is that an abstraction is treated as real entity without adequate support for this view and this is then used to support a conclusion.

This fallacy commonly occurs when abstract entities such as nature, fate and political or social entities are treated as being real entities with intentions, desires, needs and motivations of their own. Attributing such human qualities to abstractions is sometimes called the anthropomorphic fallacy or the pathetic fallacy.

This fallacy also commonly occurs when human institutions, such as states, are treated as real entities on par with (or being) natural (or supernatural) forces. This reification is often done in an attempt to justify certain actions or policies either in favor of or against the institution in question. For example, a state might be reified so as to argue that it must be obeyed. As another example, a person who pirates software, music, movies and eBooks might reify companies to argue that his theft is not morally wrong.

What counts as reification can be a matter of significant philosophical debate. This is because thinkers have, over the centuries, argued for the reality of what some would consider abstract entities. For example, some fascists have argued that the state is a real entity (complete with a personality). To automatically dismiss such arguments would be an error. As another example, thinkers such as Aristotle and Aquinas attributed purpose to natural forces. To merely dismiss their arguments would also be an error. To show that a fallacy has been committed requires providing evidence that the abstraction in question has been assumed to be a real entity without adequate support. If a legitimate argument (or arguments) for treating an abstraction in this manner has been provided, then this argument must be engaged rather than merely dismissed as a fallacy.

Example #1
Rick: "Homosexuality only occurs in humans and only by choice. In nature, there are no homosexuals. This shows that nature is opposed to homosexuality and hates it. Therefore, homosexuality is morally wrong for what nature opposes is evil."
Emile: "I'm pretty sure there are gay animals."
Hugo: "Yes, I saw a show years ago about gay penguins. I mean, they all wear tuxes and you know who wears tuxes, right?"
Emile: "Grooms?"
Hugo: "Right. And you know what grooms do?"
Emile: "Get married."
Emile: "Spot on. Since all the penguins wear tuxes, that means they are all grooms. So penguins are totally practicing gay marriage."
Rick: "No, they are not! And if they were, they'd go to hell!"

Hugo: "Yup. And it would be extra bad for them. They are, after all, accustomed to the cold."

Emile: "Those poor dead gay penguins…"

Rick: "Don't pity them! They got what they deserved!"

Example #2

Kyle: "You know, I feel bad doing this experiment. I know they signed a release and all, but zapping them with electric shocks doesn't feel right."

Gina: "I understand. This is hard on me, too. But the experiment requires that we go on and do what we must."

Kyle: "Well, if the experiment requires me to do it, then I must. I get my $15 right?"

Gina: "Of course, the experiment always keeps its word."

Kyle: "It better. Why are you having me shock people?"

Gina: "Oh, we're doing an experiment on reification."

Kyle: "Is that a fancy term for zapping people?"

Gina: "As far as you know."

Kyle: "Zap!"

Example #3

"Why do you waste your energy trying to oppose the State? You otherwise seem to be a sensible man. You do not stick your head into a fire and try to resist its burning. You don't run out in a storm and shake your fist at the tornado. You do not try to oppose gravity. Be sensible and do not resist the State. It only wants what is best for you, so even if you could someone resist, then you would only be hurting yourself. Be sensible. Come back to the loving embrace of the State. Even now, the State will forgive you your sins."

Example #4

Lulu: "I used to feel a bit bad about liberating software, music, videos and eBooks."

Sasha: "You mean 'pirate', right?"

Lulu: "Such a harsh word. But anyway, I don't feel bad at all about it now. After all when I liberate…or pirate…stuff, I am not hurting individuals. I am just pirating from the corporation. It has plenty of money and does all kinds of bad things. So, it is fine for me to pirate from it."

Sasha: "Well, would you steal a candy bar from the corner store?"

Lulu: "No way. That would be stealing from Mr. Whipple. That would be wrong."

Sasha: "But stealing from a corporation is okay? What about the artists who create the work or the people who distribute it?"

Lulu: "Yeah, it is fine. I'm not hurting those people. I'm sticking it to the corporation."

Relativist Fallacy

Also Known as: The Subjectivist Fallacy
Description:

   The Relativist Fallacy is committed when a person rejects a claim by asserting that the claim might be true for others but is not for him/her. This sort of "reasoning" has the following form:

1. Claim X is presented.
2. Person A asserts that X may be true for others but is not true for him/her.
3. Therefore A is justified in rejecting X.

   In this context, relativism is the view that truth is relative to Z (a person, time, culture, place, etc.). This is not the view that claims will be true at different times or of different people, but the view that a claim could be true for one person and false for another at the same time.

   In many cases, when people say "that X is true for me" what they really mean is "I believe X" or "X is true about me." It is important to be quite clear about the distinction between being true about a person and being true for a person. A claim is true about a person if the claim is a statement that describes the person correctly. For example, "Bill has blue eyes" is true of Bill if Bill has blue eyes. To make a claim such as "X is true for Bill" is to say that the claim is true for Bill and that it need not be true for others. For example: "1+1=23 is true for Bill" would mean that, for Bill, 1+1 actually does equal 23, not that he merely believes that 1+1=23 (that would be "It is true of Bill that he believes 1+1=23"). Another example would be "The claim that the earth is flat is true for Bill" would mean that the earth really is flat for Bill (in other words, Bill would be in a different world than the rest of the human race). Since these situations (1+1 being 23 and the earth being flat for Bill) are extremely strange, it certainly seems that truth is not relative to individuals (although beliefs are).

   As long as truth is objective (that is, not relative to individuals), then the Relativist Fallacy is a fallacy. If there are cases in which truth is actually relative, then such reasoning need not be fallacious.

Example #1:

Jill: "Look at this, Bill. I read that people who do not get enough exercise tend to be unhealthy."

Bill: "That may be true for you, but it is not true for me."

Example #2:

Jill: "I think that so called argument you used to defend your position is terrible. After all, a fallacy hardly counts as an argument. "

Bill: "That may be true for you, but it is not true for me."

Example #3:

Bill: "Your position results in a contradiction, so I can't accept it."

Dave: "Contradictions may be bad in your Eurocentric, oppressive, logical world view, but I don't think they are bad. Therefore my position is just fine."

Slippery Slope

Also known as: The Camel's Nose

Description:

The Slippery Slope is a fallacy in which a person asserts that some event must inevitably follow from another without any argument for the inevitability of the event in question. In most cases, there are a series of steps or gradations between one event and the one in question and no reason is given as to why the intervening steps or gradations will simply be bypassed. This "argument" has the following form:

1. Event X has occurred (or will or might occur).
2. Therefore event Y will inevitably happen.

This sort of "reasoning" is fallacious because there is no reason to believe that one event must inevitably follow from another without an argument for such a claim. This is especially clear in cases in which there are a significant number of steps or gradations between one event and another.

Example #1:

We have to stop the tuition increase! The next thing you know, they'll be charging $40,000 a semester!"

Example #2:

"Europe shouldn't get involved militarily in other countries. Once the governments send in a few troops, then they will send in thousands to die."

Example #3:

"You can never give anyone a break. If you do, they'll walk all over you."

Example #4:

"We've got to stop them from banning pornographic web sites. Once they start banning that, they will never stop. Next thing you know, they will be burning all the books!"

Special Pleading

Description:

Special Pleading is a fallacy in which a person applies standards, principles, rules, etc. to others while taking herself (or those she has a special interest in) to be exempt, without providing adequate justification for the exemption. This sort of "reasoning" has the following form:

1. Person A accepts standard(s) S and applies them to others in circumstance(s) C.
2. Person A is in circumstance(s) C.
3. Therefore A is exempt from S.

The person committing Special Pleading is claiming that he is exempt from certain principles or standards yet he provides no good reason for his exemption. That this sort of reasoning is fallacious is shown by the following extreme example:

1. Barbara accepts that all murderers should be punished for their crimes.
2. Although she murdered Bill, Barbara claims she is an exception because she really would not like going to prison.
3. Therefore, the standard of punishing murderers should not be applied to her.

This is obviously a blatant case of special pleading. Since no one likes going to prison, this cannot justify the claim that Barbara alone should be exempt from punishment.

The Principle of Relevant Difference

From a philosophic standpoint, the fallacy of Special Pleading is violating a well-accepted principle, namely the Principle of Relevant Difference. According to this principle, two people can be treated differently if and only if there is a relevant difference between them. This principle is a reasonable one. After all, it would not be particularly rational to treat two people differently when there is no relevant difference between them. As an extreme case, it would be very odd for a parent to insist on making one child wear size 5 shoes and the other wear size 7 shoes when the children are both size 5.

It should be noted that the Principle of Relevant Difference does allow people to be treated differently. For example, if one employee was a slacker and the other was a very productive worker the boss would be justified in giving only the productive worker a raise. This is because the productivity of each is a relevant difference between them. Since it can be reasonable to treat people differently, there will be cases in which some people will be exempt from the usual standards. For example, if it is Bill's turn to cook dinner and Bill is very ill, it would not be a case of Special Pleading if Bill asked to be excused from making dinner (this, of course, assumes that Bill does not accept a standard that requires people to cook dinner regardless of the circumstances). In this case Bill is offering a good reason as to why he should be exempt and, most importantly, it would be a good reason for anyone who was ill and not just Bill.

While determining what counts as a legitimate basis for exemption can be a difficult task, it seems clear that claiming you are exempt because you are you does not provide such a legitimate basis. Thus, unless a clear and relevant justification for exemption can be presented, a person cannot claim to be exempt.

There are cases which are similar to instances of Special Pleading in which a person is offering at least some reason why he should be exempt but the reason is not good enough to warrant the exemption. This could be called "Failed Pleading." For example, a professor may claim to be exempt from helping the rest of the faculty move books to the new department office because it would be beneath his dignity. However, this is not a particularly good reason and would hardly justify his exemption. If it turns out that the real "reason" a person is claiming exemption is that they simply take themselves to be exempt, then they would be committing Special Pleading. Such cases will be fairly common. After all, it is fairly rare for adults to simply claim they are exempt without at least some pretense of justifying the exemption.

Example #1

Bill and Jill are married. Both Bill and Jill have put in a full day at the office. Their dog, Rover, has knocked over all the plants in one room and has strewn the dirt all over the carpet. When they return, Bill tells Jill that it is her job to clean up after the dog. When she protests, he says that he has put in a full day at the office and is too tired to clean up after the dog.

Example #2

Jane and Sue share a dorm room.

Jane: "Turn of that stupid stereo, I want to take a nap."
Sue: 'Why should I? What are you exhausted or something?"
Jane: "No, I just feel like taking a nap."
Sue: "Well, I feel like playing my stereo."
Jane: "Well, I'm taking my nap. You have to turn your stereo off and that's final."

Example #3

Mike and Barbara share an apartment.

Mike: "Barbara, you've tracked in mud again."
Barbara: "So? It's not my fault."
Mike: "Sure. I suppose it walked in on its own. You made the mess, so you clean it up."
Barbara: "Why?"
Mike: "We agreed that whoever makes a mess has to clean it up. That is fair."
Barbara: "Well, I'm going to watch TV. If you don't like the mud, then you clean it up."
Mike: "Barbara..."
Barbara: "What? I want to watch the show. I don't want to clean up the mud. Like I said, if it bothers you that much, then you should clean it up."

Spotlight

Description:

The Spotlight fallacy is committed when a person uncritically assumes that all members or cases of a certain class or type are like those that receive the most attention or coverage in the media. This line of "reasoning" has the following form:

1. Xs with quality Q receive a great deal of attention or coverage in the media.
2. Therefore all Xs have quality Q.

This line of reasoning is fallacious since the mere fact that someone or something attracts the most attention or coverage in the media does not mean that it automatically represents the whole population. For example, suppose a mass murderer from Old Town, Maine received a great deal of attention in the media. It would hardly follow that everyone from the town is a mass murderer.

The Spotlight fallacy derives its name from the fact that receiving a great deal of attention or coverage is often referred to as being in the spotlight. It is similar to Hasty Generalization, Biased Sample and Misleading Vividness because the error being made involves generalizing about a population based on an inadequate or flawed sample.

The Spotlight Fallacy is a very common fallacy. This fallacy most often occurs when people assume that those who receive the most media attention actually represent the groups they belong to. For example, some people began to believe that all those who oppose abortion are willing to gun down doctors in cold blood simply because those incidents received a great deal of media attention. Since the media typically covers people or events that are unusual or exceptional, it is somewhat odd for people to believe that such people or events are representative.

For brief discussions of adequate samples and generalizations, see the entries for Hasty Generalization and Biased Sample.

Example #1:
Bill: "Jane, you say you are a feminist, but you can't be."
Jane: "What! What do you mean? Is this one of your stupid jokes or something?"
Bill: "No, I'm serious. Over the summer I saw feminists appear on several talk shows and news shows and I read about them in the papers. The women were really bitter and said that women were victims of men and needed to be given special compensation. You are always talking about equal rights and forging your own place in the world. So, you can't be a feminist."
Jane: "Bill, there are many types of feminism, not just the brands that get media attention."
Bill: "Oh. Sorry."

Example #2:
Joe: "Man, I'd never want to go to New York. It is all concrete and pollution."
Sam: "Not all of it."
Joe: "Sure it is. Every time I watch the news they are always showing concrete, skyscrapers, and lots of pollution."
Sam: "Sure, that is what the news shows, but a lot of New York is farmlands and forest. It is not all New York City, it just receives most of the attention."

Example #3:
Ann: "I'm not letting little Jimmy use his online account anymore!"
Sasha: "Why not? Did he hack into the Pentagon and try to start world war three?"

Ann: "No. Haven't you been watching the news and reading the papers? There are perverts online just waiting to molest kids! You should take away your daughter's account. Why, there must be thousands of sickos out there!"

Sasha: "Really? I thought that there were only a very few cases."

Ann: "I'm not sure of the exact number, but if the media is covering it so much , then most people who are online must be indecent."

Straw Man

Description:

The Straw Man fallacy is committed when a person simply ignores a person's actual position and substitutes a distorted, exaggerated or misrepresented version of that position. This sort of "reasoning" has the following pattern:

1. Person A has position X.
2. Person B presents position Y (which is a distorted version of X).
3. Person B attacks position Y.
4. Therefore X is false/incorrect/flawed.

This sort of "reasoning" is fallacious because attacking a distorted version of a position simply does not constitute an attack on the position itself. One might as well expect an attack on a poor drawing of a person to hurt the person.

Example #1

Prof. Jones: "The university just cut our yearly budget by $10,000."

Prof. Smith: "What are we going to do?"

Prof. Brown: "I think we should eliminate one of the teaching assistant positions. That would take care of it."

Prof. Jones: "We could reduce our scheduled raises instead."

Prof. Brown:" I can't understand why you want to bleed us dry like that, Jones."

Example #2

"Senator Jones says that we should not fund the attack submarine program. I disagree entirely. I can't understand why he wants to leave us defenseless like that."

Example #3

Bill and Jill are arguing about cleaning out their closets:

Jill: "We should clean out the closets. They are getting a bit messy."

Bill: "Why, we just went through those closets last year. Do we have to clean them out every day?"

Jill: I never said anything about cleaning them out every day. You just want too keep all your junk forever, which is just ridiculous."

Texas Sharpshooter Fallacy

Also Known as: Sharpshooter Fallacy

Description:

This fallacy occurs when it is concluded that a cluster in a set of data must be the result of a cause (typically whatever the cluster is clustered around). This fallacy has the following form:

1. A cluster L occurs in data set D around C.
2. Therefore C is the cause of L.

This causal fallacy occurs because the conclusion is drawn without properly considering alternatives. One alternative that is ignored is the possibility that the cluster is the result of chance rather than an actual causal factor. Another alternative that is ignored is that the cluster might be the result of a cause, but not the claimed causal factor.

A cluster does provide grounds for considering a causal hypothesis that can then be properly tested. However, mere correlation does not establish causation. Given the role that correlation (in this case, clustering) plays, this fallacy can be considered a specific variation of the cum hoc ergo propter hoc fallacy. However, Texas sharpshooter has a history of its own that warrants its inclusion under its own name.

The fallacy's name is derived from a joke about a person (usually a Texan) who shoots away at the broad side of a barn. He then paints a target around the biggest cluster of bullet holes and claims to be a sharpshooter. This creates the illusion that he is a good shot, just as focusing on clusters and ignoring the rest of the data can create the impression of a causal connection. As such, this fallacy can also be seen as very similar to incomplete evidence in that when a person "draws the target" what is outside the target is conveniently ignored. Since Texas sharpshooter is specifically a causal fallacy, it can be distinguished from the more general fallacy of incomplete evidence in this way.

Example #1

Rich: "Hmm, this data shows that the number of cases of cancer in Old Town is greater than the national average."

Alice: "Interesting. Do you have any data that is more precise?"

Rich: "Indeed, take a look at this graphic. As you can see, it shows a significant clustering of cases near the paper mill."

Alice: "Wow! Those poor people!"

Rich: "You know makes it really bad?"

Alice: "What?"

Rich: "The housing around the mill is for retired senior citizens!"

Alice: "Wait, what?"

Example #2

Michelle: "I was reading through the predictions of Nostradamus. He must have been able to see the future because his predictions came true."

Hilda: "What did he get right?"

Michelle: "Well, he predicted Hitler. He said 'Beasts wild with hunger will cross the rivers, The greater part of the battle will be against Hister. He will cause great men to be dragged in a cage of iron, When the son of Germany obeys no law.'"

Hilda: "Wow, that is amazing! 'Hister' is really close to 'Hitler', he was German...well close enough anyway and he did cross rivers."

Michelle: "Like I said, he made those predictions because he could see the future."

Hilda: "Did all his predictions come true? That book you have looks pretty thick."

Michelle: "Well, he did write hundreds of predictions and only a few have come true. But, he was seeing the future so it will take a while for them all to come true. The important thing is that he got Hitler and some other things right so far!"

Fran: "You know that 'Hister' is just the Latin name for the Danube river, right? Also, your translation is a bit off. In any case..."

Michelle: "Shut up!"

Two Wrongs Make a Right

Description:

Two Wrongs Make a Right is a fallacy in which a person "justifies" an action against a person by asserting that the person would do the same thing to him/her, when the action is not necessary to prevent B from doing X to A. This fallacy has the following pattern of "reasoning":

1. It is claimed that person B would do X to person A.
2. It is acceptable for person A to do X to person B (when A's doing X to B is not necessary to prevent B from doing X to A).

This sort of "reasoning" is fallacious because an action that is wrong is wrong even if another person would also do it.

It should be noted that it can be the case that it is not wrong for A to do X to B if X is done to prevent B from doing X to A or if X is done in justified retribution. For example, if Sally is running in the park and Biff tries to attack her, Sally would be justified in attacking Biff to defend herself. As another example, if country A is planning to invade country B in order to enslave the people, then country B would be justified in launching a preemptive strike to prevent the invasion.

Example #1:
Bill has borrowed Jane's expensive pen, but found he didn't return it. He tells himself that it is okay to keep it, since she would have taken his.

Example #2:
Jane: "Did you hear about those terrorists killing those poor people? That sort of killing is just wrong."
Sue: "Those terrorists are justified. After all, their land was taken from them. It is morally right for them to do what they do."
Jane: "Even when they blow up busloads of children?"
Sue: "Yes. "

Example #3:
After leaving a bookstore, Jill notices that she was undercharged for her book. She decides not to return the money to the store because if she had overpaid, they would not have returned the money."

Example #4:
Jill is horrified by the way the state uses capital punishment. Bill says that capital punishment is fine, since those the state kill don't have any qualms about killing others.

Victim Fallacy

Description:

This fallacy occurs when a person uncritically assumes that the cause of a perceived mistreatment (such as not being hired or receiving a poor grade) is due to prejudice (such as sexism or racism) on the part of the person or persons involved in the perceived mistreatment. The form of "reasoning" is as follows:

1. Person P believes s/he is being mistreated by person or persons M.
2. Person P regards himself or herself as a member of group G and believes this group has been subject to prejudice. Or P believes that M regards him/her as a member of G.
3. P uncritically concludes that his/her perceived mistreatment is the result of prejudice against G on the part of M.

This is a fallacy because the mere that that a person perceives himself or herself as being mistreated does not provide sufficient justification for the claim that the alleged mistreatment is the result of prejudice. After all, even if the situation does involve mistreatment, it might be the result of factors that have nothing to do with prejudice of the sort being considered. For example, imagine the following situation: Jane is taking a chemistry class and always comes to class late, disrupting the lecture when she strolls in. She also blatantly checks her text messages on her mobile phone during class. She earns a B in the class, but is assigned a C instead because the professor is angry about her behavior. Jane would be correct to conclude she has been mistreated given the disparity between what she earned and what she received, but she would not be justified in assuming that it was "just because she was a woman" without adequate evidence for the professor being a sexist.

This mistake is reasoning is similar to the various causal fallacies. In these fallacies an uncritical leap is made from insufficient evidence to conclude that one thing caused another. In this case, a leap is being made without sufficient evidence to conclude that the alleged mistreatment was caused by prejudice.

Reasonably concluding that an alleged mistreatment is the result of prejudice involves establishing that the mistreatment is, in fact, a mistreatment and the most plausible explanation for the mistreatment is prejudice. Without taking these steps, the person is engaging in poor reasoning and is not justified in his/her conclusion- even if the conclusion is, in fact, true. This is because good reasoning is not just about getting a correct conclusion (this could be done accidentally by guessing) but by getting it in the right way.

If a person has good reason to believe that the alleged mistreatment is a mistreatment and that it is a result of prejudice, then the reasoning would obviously not be fallacious. For example, if Jane was aware that she earned a B and was intentionally assigned a C, she would be justified in believing she was mistreated. If the professor made sexist remarks and Jane knew he downgraded other women in the class and none of the men, then Jane would be justified in concluding that the mistreatment stemmed from prejudice.

Not surprisingly, the main factor that leads people to commit this fallacy "honestly" is because the group in question has been subject to prejudice. From a psychological standpoint, it is natural for a person who is aware of prejudice against the group in question to perceive mistreatment as coming from that prejudice. And, as a matter of fact, when considering a perceived mistreatment it would be quite reasonable to consider the possibility of prejudice. However, until there is adequate evidence it remains just that-a mere possibility.

In addition to cases in which the fallacy is committed as an honest mistake, there are cases in which this type of "reasoning" is cynically exploited as an excuse or even as a means of revenge (charges of prejudice, even if completely unfounded, can do a lot of damage to a person's career in many professions). As an example of an excuse, a person who has done poorly in a class because of a lack of effort might tell his parents that "the professor has this thing against men."

In addition to the fact that this is a mistake in reasoning, there are other reasons to avoid this fallacy. First, uncritically assuming that other people are prejudiced is itself a sign of prejudice. For example, to uncritically assume that all whites are racists is just as racist as assuming that all Jewish people are covetous or all blacks are criminals. Second, use of this fallacy, especially as the "reasoning" behind an excuse can have serious consequences. For example, if a student who did poorly in a class because of a lack of effort concludes that his grade was the result of racism and tells his parents, they might consider a law suit against the professor. As another example, if a person becomes accustomed to being able to fall back on this line of "reasoning" they might be less motivated in their efforts since they can "explain" their failures through prejudice.

It must be emphasized that it is not being claimed that prejudice does not really exist or that people are not victims of prejudice. It is being claimed that people need to be very carefully in their reasoning when it comes to prejudice and accusations of prejudice.

Example #1

Sam: "Can you believe this-I got a C in that class."
Jane: "Well, your work was pretty average and you didn't put much effort into the class. How often did you show up, anyway?"

Sam: "That has nothing to do with it. I deserve at least a B. That chick teaching the class just hates men. That's why I did badly."

Bill: "Hey, I earned an 'A', man."

Sam: "She just likes you because you're not a real man like me."

Example #2

Ricardo: "I applied for six jobs and got turned down six times!"

Ann: "Where did you apply?"

Ricardo: "Six different software companies."

Ann: "What did you apply for?"

Ricardo: "Programming jobs to develop apps for Android.

Ann: "But you majored in philosophy and haven't programmed anything. Is that why you didn't get the jobs?"

Ricardo: "No. All the people interviewing me were white or Asian. A person like me just can't get a job in the white and yellow world of technology."

Example #3

Dave: "Can you believe that-those people laughed at me when I gave my speech."

Will: "Well, that was cruel. But you really should make sure that you have your facts right before giving a speech. As two examples, Plato was not an Italian and Descartes did not actually say 'I drink, therefore I am.'"

Dave: "They wouldn't have laughed if a straight guy had said those things!"

Will: "Really?"

Dave: "Yeah! They laughed just because I'm gay!"

Will: "Well, they didn't laugh at me, but I actually did my research."

Dave: "Maybe they just don't know you're gay."

Will: "Yeah, that must be it."

Weak Analogy

Also Known As: False Analogy, Fallacious Analogical Argument

Description:

This fallacy occurs when an analogical argument is not strong enough for its premises to adequately support its conclusion. The fallacy of weak analogy has the same form as the analogical argument. The fallaciousness occurs not because of the form but because the specific argument fails to meet the conditions of a strong analogical argument.

Strictly presented, an analogical argument will have three premises and a conclusion. The first two premises (attempt to) establish the analogy by showing that the things in question are similar in certain respects. The third premise establishes the additional fact known about one thing and the conclusion asserts that because the two things are alike in other respects, they are alike in this additional respect as well.

Although people generally present analogical arguments in a fairly informal manner, they have the following logical form:

1. Premise 1: X has properties P,Q, and R.
2. Premise 2: Y has properties P,Q, and R.
3. Premise 3: X has property Z as well.
4. Conclusion: Y has property Z.

X and Y are variables that stand for whatever is being compared, such as chimpanzees and humans or blood and money. P, Q, R, and Z are also variables, but they stand for properties or qualities, such as having a heart or being essential for survival. The use of P, Q, and R is just for the sake of the illustration-the things being compared might have many more properties in common.

An example of a non-fallacious analogical argument presented in strict form is as follows:

Premise 1: Rats are mammals and possess a nervous system that includes a developed brain.
Premise 2: Humans are mammals possess a nervous system that includes a developed brain.
Premise 3: When exposed to Nerve Agent 274, 90% of the rats died.
Conclusion: If exposed to Nerve Agent 274, 90% of all humans will die.

The strength of an analogical argument depends on three factors. To the degree that an analogical argument meets these standards it is a strong argument. If an analogical argument fails to meet these standards, then it is weak. If it is weak enough, then it would be considered fallacious. There is no exact point at which an analogical argument becomes fallacious, however the standards do provide an objective basis for making this assessment.

First, the more properties X and Y have in common, the better the argument. For example, in the example given above rats and humans have many properties in common. This standard is based on the common sense notion that the more two things are alike in other ways, the more likely it is that they will be alike in some other way. It should be noted that even if the two things are very much alike in many respects, there is still the possibility that they are not alike in regards to Z. This is why analogical arguments are inductive.

Second, the more relevant the shared properties are to property Z, the stronger the argument. A specific property, for example P, is relevant to property Z if the presence or absence of P affects the likelihood that Z will be present. Using the example, above, the shared properties are relevant. After all, since nerve agents work on the nervous system, the presence of a nervous system makes it more likely that something will be killed by such agents. It should be kept in mind that it is possible for X and Y to share relevant properties while Y does not actually have property Z. Again, this is part of the reason why analogical arguments are inductive.

Third, it must be determined whether X and Y have relevant dissimilarities as well as similarities. The more dissimilarities and the more relevant they are, the weaker the argument. In the example above, humans and rats do have dissimilarities, but most of them are probably not particularly relevant to the effects of nerve agents. However, it would be worth considering that the size difference might be relevant-at the dosage the rats received, humans might be less likely to die. Thus, size would be a difference worth considering.

Example #1
"The flow of electricity through wires is like the flowing of water through pipes. Water flows faster downhill, so electricity does, too. This, by the way, is why electrical wires are run on poles-that way the electricity can flow quickly into your house."

Example #2
Glenn: "Obama is going to do the same things to America that Hitler did to Germany!"
Bill: "What?"
Glenn: "Obama was democratically elected. So was Hitler. Do I need to bust out some chalk and draw it out for you?"
Bill: "Sure."
Glenn: "I'm out of chalk."
Bill: "Too bad."

Example #3
Steve: "Those darn Republicans!"
Lena: "How have they hurt your liberal sensibilities this time?"
Steve: "They are saying that the health care plan is a big government takeover. They are making a big lie, just like Goebbels did. It is just like blood libel."
Lena: "That seems to be a bit much."

Steve: "Not at all. You know, that is how the Holocaust got started. With a big lie. The Republicans are going to cause a Holocaust because they are just like the Nazis!"

Lena: "That is quite a comparison."

Steve: "I know!"

Formal (Deductive) Fallacies

As noted in the introduction, a formal (or deductive) fallacy is an invalid deductive argument. An invalid deductive argument is one that *can* have all true premises and a false conclusion at the same time. It is this quality that makes all invalid deductive arguments fallacious (although some authors prefer to exclude such invalid arguments from being deductive arguments). Interestingly enough, an invalid deductive argument can actually have all true premises and a true conclusion. The problem with an invalid argument is that the reasoning is defective. Of course, an invalid argument can also have false premises and a false conclusion, but this has nothing to do with its invalidity.

Unlike the informal fallacies presented above, there are clear and objective tests to determine whether a deductive argument is invalid (fallacious) or not. These methods include truth tables, proofs, Venn diagrams and other means that go beyond the intended scope of this work.

However, if an argument form is invalid it is always invalid. Likewise, if an argument form is valid, that form is always valid. So, if you know some valid and invalid forms, you will be able to spot those good and bad arguments.

In theory, there are an infinite number of invalid arguments. Fortunately, there are only a few formal fallacies that are common enough to be named. They often trick people because they are "evil twins" of valid arguments that are also common enough to be named. Three of the common formal fallacies are given below along with their good twins.

Affirming the Consequent

This argument is an "evil twin" of the valid argument affirming the antecedent (more formally known as modus ponens)

Affirming the Consequent (Invalid)
Premise 1: If P, Then Q
Premise 2: Q
Conclusion: P

Affirming the Antecedent (Valid)
Premise 1: If P, Then Q
Premise 2: P
Conclusion: Q

Example #1
Premise 1: If Sally had seen Star Wars episode IV, then she would know who Darth Vader is.
Premise 2: Sally knows who Darth Vader is.
Conclusion: So, Sally has seen Star Wars episode IV.

Example #2
Premise 1: If Ted gets a 60 on the final, then he will pass the class.
Premise 2: Ted passed the class.
Conclusion: Ted got a 60 on the final.

Example #3
Premise 1: If Sally is a socialist, then she is in favor of national health care.
Premise 2: Sally is in favor of national health care.
Conclusion: Sally is a socialist.

Denying the Antecedent

This argument is an "evil twin" of the valid argument denying the consequent (more formally known as modus tollens).

Denying the Antecedent (Invalid)
Premise 1: If P, then Q.
Premise 2: Not P
Conclusion: Not Q

Denying the Consequent (Valid)
Premise 1: If P, then Q.
Premise 2: Not Q
Conclusion: Not P

Example #1
Premise 1: If Sally buys *Halo 4*, then she can play *Halo 4*.
Premise 2: Sally did not buy *Halo 4*.
Conclusion: Sally cannot play *Halo 4*

Example #2
Premise 1: If Sam gets a 60 on the final, then he passes the class.
Premise 2: Sam did not get a 60 on the final.
Conclusion: Sam did not pass the class.

Example #3
Premise 1: If the dog had eaten the cake, the cake would be gone.
Premise 2: The dog did not eat the cake.
Conclusion: The cake is not gone.

Undistributed Middle

This argument is an "evil twin" of the valid argument hypothetical syllogism (also sometimes known as chain argument).

Undistributed Middle (Invalid)
Premise 1: If P, then Q.
Premise 2: If R, then Q
Conclusion: If P, then R

Hypothetical Syllogism/Chain Argument (Valid)
Premise 1: If P, then Q.
Premise 2: If Q, then R
Conclusion: If P, then R

Example #1
Premise 1: If you eat fish, then you are a carnivore.
Premise 2: If you are an omnivore, you are also a carnivore.
Conclusion: So, if you eat fish, you are an omnivore.

Example #2
Premise 1: If Bill passes the final, then he will pass the class.
Premise 2: If Bill gets a 100 on the final, then he will pass the class.
Conclusion: If Bill passes the final, then he will get a 100 on the final.

Example #3
Premise 1: If Fenris is a wolf, then he is a mammal.
Premise 2: If Morris is a cat, then he is a mammal.
Conclusion: If Fenris is a wolf, then Morris is a cat.

Other Philosophy Books by the Author

42 Fallacies

30 More Fallacies

For Better & Worse Reasoning

Moral Methods

Philosophical Provocations Volume 1

Philosophical Provocations Volume 2

Envy & Class Warfare

A Six-Gun for Socrates

CPSIA information can be obtained
at www.ICGtesting.com
Printed in the USA
LVHW08s2311040918
589186LV00012B/78/P